ENHANCING READING COMPREHENSION
in the Language Learning Classroom

TAMAR FEUERSTEIN
MIRIAM SCHCOLNIK

Alta Book Center, Publishers
San Francisco, California USA

ALTA TEACHER RESOURCE SERIES

Project Editor	Aarón Berman Sonoma State University, California USA Alta Book Center, Publishers
Consulting Editor	Jean Zukowski/Faust Northern Arizona University USA
Content Editor	Margaret Walworth Gallaudet University, Washington, D.C. USA
Design/Production	Cleve Gallat, CTA Graphics, San Francisco USA
Illustrations	Agur Schiff Iris Rilov
Icon Designs	Addy Feuerstein

© 1995 Alta Book Center, Publishers
San Francisco, California 94010 USA

Printed in the United States of America

ISBN 1-882483-27-8

Contents

▶ ▶

Preface

▶ ▶

In today's world, one of the most important ways to communicate with speakers of other languages and with members of other cultures is via reading. Reading comprehension is, therefore, a major objective of second and foreign language instruction.

Reading comprehension has been the focus of many research studies in the last decade. As a result, reading comprehension is viewed, to date, as a communicative, interactive, procedural approach to the study of text. In this process, readers and writers interact through the written text and no text can be fully perceived as an entity of meaning without the reader's interpretation of that meaning. It is therefore imperative that in the language classroom we help learners develop their individual reading strategies. It is for this reason that I consider this book so very important for all language teachers both as a friendly guide and a useful resource.

New and exciting reading materials keep appearing on the market almost daily, and universities, teacher colleges, and other teacher training institutions have developed excellent courses to deal with the teaching of reading comprehension. Yet, when it comes down to it, the classroom teacher is left with the enormous task of adapting all these materials and ideas to his/her particular class. This book can help the teacher in the daily decision-making process within the reading comprehension lesson and across the reading comprehension curriculum.

In dealing with the skill of reading, the course designer and the materials developer must synthesize various elements: a) theories about the nature of reading itself, specifically models of adult reading in one's first language; b) the specific characteristics and needs of second-language readers; c) the features of reading selections through textual analysis. The purpose of this book is to help teachers use these three different aspects of the reading skill in choosing, developing and using reading and learning activities in the second/foreign language classroom. Teachers using this book will find that each chapter in the book guides them through the most important theoretical considerations towards the most practical classroom solutions for their particular group of students. It was a great pleasure to have had the opportunity to encourage Tamar and Miriam in the development and the production of this very welcomed resource book for language teachers at all levels.

Elite Olshtain

School of Education
Hebrew University
Jerusalem, January 1994

Introduction

▶ ▶

This book is intended for foreign and second language in-service and pre-service teachers. It deals with reading comprehension skills and strategies needed by language learners. The sample activities in the book are suitable for a variety of populations and levels, and all activities can be adapted to a variety of needs. Although the activities are in English, they are easily applicable to other foreign or second language situations. Text based activities can be easily modified and adapted to suit other texts in English or another language.

As a teacher, you will have to select and sequence the materials that are appropriate to your particular student population. Sometimes you will have to adapt them to your students' specific needs as well as make decisions about the mode of presentation.

Use this book as a resource. The activities in it are meant as samples. You may use the activities suggested as they are or modify them to suit your needs. You may decide that an activity is inappropriate for you and skip it altogether.

AIMS AND ORGANIZATION OF THIS BOOK

The aim of this book is to provide an orderly presentation of the most common reading skills and strategies, to give a brief explanation of each, and then to suggest class activities and procedures to make students aware of the various reading processes. Chapter One deals with traditional and current approaches to reading comprehension. Chapter Two deals with the reading comprehension lesson and suggests general sequences and techniques. Chapter Three deals with dictionary skills. Chapter Four presents ideas for dealing with information that is outside the text. Chapters Five through Eight are devoted to discussing specific reading strategies. An appendix, glossary, and index follow Chapter Eight. We grouped reading strategies into four main categories:

1. Heuristic processes—processes that involve guessing, predicting, or inferring.

2. Processes of analysis—strategies necessary for analyzing a text.

3. Processes of unification or cohesion—processes that allow readers to grasp the logical organization and connections in a text.

4. Processes of evaluation—processes that allow readers to read critically and be aware of the writer's point of view.

Chapter One

▶ ▶

Overview

**TRADITIONAL APPROACHES TO TEACHING
READING COMPREHENSION**

The traditional classroom approach to reading comprehension sees the product—the correct answer—as the end. The student is expected to understand and sometimes remember factual information provided by a text. A reader might be expected, for example, to answer questions such as "Whom did John meet? When? Where?" Sometimes the text is used merely as a context for grammatical structures. Such a text is likely to be followed by an instruction like this: "Find examples of the present perfect in the story and explain their use."

At other times, the text is the basis for activities that demand going beyond the text. These activities traditionally deal with some moral issue, the message of the text, or call for reader involvement. Discussion of a moral issue might include the question "In your opinion, is John's behavior justified?" When the message is the object of emphasis, the question is "What do we learn from this story?" If the purpose of the activity is reader involvement or judgment, the questions could be "Would you do the same thing if you were in John's position? What would you say to Mary?"

All these activities have a place in teaching reading— especially at the early stages of reading in a foreign or second language, when the vocabulary and the grammatical structures available to the student are limited and limiting. However, it is worthwhile examining this practice a little closer. To focus on this, try the short exercise that follows.

Although the following is a nonsense text, it is based on a passage from a real textbook. The format has not been changed, and the sequence of activities is true to the original. As you answer the questions, pretend you are a student. The exercise is short, so it should not take you more than 5 minutes.

Read the following text carefully.

> **The quirty charns knagged the forik fobes chirpily. Therefore, the fobes tored the charns. They also renked the birry boke.**

Use full sentences to answer the following questions.
1. Who knagged chirpily?
2. What did the quirty charns do?
3. How did they do it?
4. How did the forik fobes react?
5. Did the forik fobes do anything else?
6. What did they do?
7. Who renked the birry boke?
8. In your opinion, did the birry boke deserve it? Why?
9. Why did the fobes tore the charns?
10. Discuss the reason for the fobes' behavior.

 ▶▶▶ INSIGHTS ◀◀◀

Notice that questions 1 through 7 asked about factual information. We are sure that you had no difficulty answering them.

Questions 8 through 9 asked for opinions. Question 10 is a typical homework assignment and is, therefore, at the end of the series. Questions 8 through 10 probably took a little longer to do than the others but were still quite easy.

What are the implications of this exercise? Obviously, the fact that you could answer the questions does not reflect real comprehension, because the text is nonsensical. How were you able to answer them?

You relied first and foremost on your knowledge of similar text types and similar textbook activities. The syntax was all there, and the function words were familiar. You worked within a familiar framework. You, as a good student, had developed strategies for coping with activities of this sort. You could manipulate the text in a way that allowed you to answer questions mechanically. You applied familiar strategies to a new text. But did you exhibit reading comprehension? Did the activity demand any comprehension at all?

Take a look at the nonsense story again. These types of questions often follow reading comprehension exercises.

The quirty charns knagged the forik fobes chirpily. Therefore, the fobes tored the charns. They also renked the birry boke.

Language and Structure:
1. What part of speech are the following words?
   quirty, charns, knagged, forik, forbes, chirpily, tored, renked, birry, boke
2. Turn the following adjectives into adverbs. Pay particular attention to spelling rules.
   quirty, forik, birry
3. Rewrite the story in the present progressive tense.
4. Rewrite the story in the simple present tense, singular. Don't forget to make all the necessary changes!
5. Rewrite each sentence so it is in the passive voice.

You have probably drawn your own conclusions already. Did you notice that the activities did not teach you anything? All the knowledge was yours! You were tested, not taught. In other words, when we demand that students deal with a similar sequence of activities, we demand a lot from them. The cognitive load is very high. We do not help them in the process. We demand that they cope with all the difficulties on their own and that they apply a host of rules and strategies. When they fail, we place the blame on them. In most cases, we demand that they do the reading over again until they are proficient. In some cases, the procedure works. After all, most of us have learned to read with comprehension. But, in many others, this product-focused approach fails.

CURRENT APPROACHES TO TEACHING READING COMPREHENSION

Current theories of reading emphasize the cognitive processes the reader employs to read with comprehension. These theories assume that readers develop certain mental abilities that allow them to process texts. This is the approach we wish to demonstrate in the present book.

Current approaches to reading comprehension emphasize the *process* of reading rather than the product. In other words, rather than focusing on students' performance after reading, current approaches focus on what the reader actually does while reading. Process is viewed as an interaction between reader and text. The reader contributes his or her background knowledge—that is, linguistic knowledge and general world knowledge. The text provides new information which will eventually become part of the reader's stock of knowledge.

Readers employ a great number of cognitive skills and strate-gies. These strategies facilitate the reader's interaction with the text. They help readers make the proper logical connections, ana-lyze the text, and put the elements together. In other words, the process of reading involves sampling portions of the text, making the necessary connections, making hypotheses about subsequent sections, and testing these hypotheses against the text.

Our ultimate goal in teaching reading skills and strategies is their internalization and the students' increased ability to transfer strategies from one reading text to another. Our basic assumption is that, by teaching certain reading skills and strategies, we will help students develop procedures that will enable them to read with better comprehension. Reading strategies may be naturally activated in the students' first language, but not transferred to the second language. On the other hand, they may never have been activated. In either case, activating these strategies is beneficial because that brings awareness of skills previously acquired in the first language and allows students to practice the skills and strate-gies that they have not yet internalized.

WHAT DO GOOD READERS DO?

Research in both first and second languages teaches us a lot about the good reader. We know, for example, that good readers are good decoders. That means they recognize words, expressions, and phrases accurately. It also means that they need fewer guess-ing strategies than poor readers. When readers are not good at decoding, they rely heavily on guessing and often make wrong guesses. Their guesses depend on previous knowledge, on text type, and familiarity with texts of that type.

We also know that good readers have a large repertoire of strategies available to them. They can shift strategies during the reading process. They can abandon unsuccessful strategies, try new strategies that are appropriate, and re-employ previously used strategies when necessary. They are also able to combine strategies so that their reading becomes fluent and meaningful.

Good readers make effective use of the text. They notice contextual information at the local level and at the global level. They are therefore able to notice inconsistencies, repetitions, redundancies, and changes in mood, tone, and argument.

PROBLEMS THAT FOREIGN- OR SECOND-LANGUAGE READERS ENCOUNTER

Foreign- or second-language readers encounter a host of problems. The most obvious are text-based. Learners unfamiliar with the Roman alphabet have a decoding deficiency that results in slow reading. Slow reading in itself can be regarded as a deficiency. It may result in inaccurate reading because the reader can lose the connections and have difficulty understanding the text as a whole.

Some students have numerous linguistic deficiencies. They often lack vocabulary, or they may know a word but with a different meaning. Students usually perceive vocabulary as the most serious difficulty they have. They may be unfamiliar with grammatical structures as well. These deficiencies may lead students to inaccurate reading, which results in erroneous interpretation.

Lack of practice is probably the most serious source of reading difficulties. The more a student reads, the more proficient he or she becomes. The typical foreign- or second- language learner lacks practice and, as a result, encounters difficulties in reading.

As language teachers, we should strive to motivate our students to read more. Practice and suitable materials will make reading an enjoyable experience.

EXTENSIVE READING

Extensive reading implies reading individually and silently for the purpose of enjoyment. In other words, the teacher is not directly involved in the process. Extensive reading can take place outside school. The main task for the teacher, then, is to motivate the process, to make students want to read, and to help whenever needed.

Extensive reading is very important. Some claim that it is the most important activity in the acquisition of reading comprehension. One learns reading by reading and, the more one reads, the better reader one becomes. Readers who enjoy reading read faster and have fewer problems than those who don't. As a result, they also read more. Since they read more, their comprehension improves and their enjoyment increases.

Poor readers and unmotivated readers, on the other hand, find it difficult to comprehend what they read, and their process of reading is slow and tedious. As a result, they do not enjoy reading, and they read less. Poor readers need more of the teacher's attention. They are the ones who need to be motivated.

It is not enough to assign extensive reading. The discussion that follows may help you motivate your students and create a whole class of readers.

The Choice of Texts: Simplified Versus Nonsimplified Materials

Researchers still debate whether simplified texts are the solution for foreign or second language learners. No doubt simplified texts are easier to read, but they do present problems.

Some experts claim that processing a simplified text is not genuine reading. They question the need for simplified texts by asserting that there is no need to understand everything presented. Moreover, simplified texts, as a rule, are less interesting to read. When novels are simplified for the foreign language student, the story line usually remains, but situations, descriptions, and secondary characters are changed or removed altogether. In most cases the language of the author is stripped of its unique features. Vocabulary is simplified and controlled, sentences are shortened, and complex language structures are removed. One striking feature of simplified texts is that they leave very little to the imagination. The most sensitive readers are likely to find explicit text unattractive. As a rule, the simpler the text is, the more explicit it is.

Researchers claim, therefore, that simplified texts can be more difficult to process than nonsimplified texts. For example, simplified texts often lack cohesive markers. Leaving out words reduces sentence length, but it increases comprehension difficulty. The consequence of simplification may be a choppy, unnatural text.

In addition, those who read simplified texts become used to controlled vocabularies. They become accustomed to reading simple sentences that are rare in academic writing. In other words, they are denied exposure to the more complex language that is probably more useful for their academic pursuits. Some researchers suggest that elaboration—that is, adding explanations and clarifying concepts within the text—may be more appropriate for language-learning readers than simplification.

Authentic reading materials may be more difficult to read, but they allow students to assess how much they really understand. In addition, they expose students to new grammar and vocabulary. Authentic reading material must be selected with caution, however, because material that is very difficult will discourage the student and could result in less reading.

SUGGESTIONS FOR PRACTICE

The following suggestions do not depend on the book you select. Some of the activities are designed to motivate students; others relate to specific teaching points.

Entire Class Reads the Same Book

If you decide to have the whole class read the same book, try one or more of these activities:

- In class, predict the contents of the book from the title, subtitle, or chapter titles. If the book is illustrated, students can use pictures as the basis for predictions. Periodically compare students' guesses with actual events.
- Read the beginnings or endings of chapters together.
- Use the book as a source of vocabulary enrichment. Have students write their own lists and then test one another. (The

students' quizzes should be very short. Suggest formats to your students.)

▶ Ask students to suggest questions or brief activities that arise out of the reading. Grade students on the merit of the activities that they suggest. Select the best activities and do them in class.

▶ Ask students to prepare advertisements that encourage others to read a particular book. Display the ads around the room. Provide time for other students to view them.

▶ A week before students are supposed to have finished reading, take time to allow students to suggest various endings to the story.

Individuals or Groups Read Different Books

If students work individually or in small groups, use one or more of these activities:

▶ Ask each student to try to persuade others to read a book. Suggest that class members prepare forms that praise what they have read. A sample form follows.

Title of book:

Author:

I enjoyed reading this book because . . .

_____

I recommend this book because . . .

_____

I am sure you will enjoy reading this book because . . .

_____

I will read this book within the next ___ weeks/ months.

Signature:_____

If appropriate, offer prizes to those who "sell" books to the largest number of readers.

- Have a session in which students can share their impressions of what they have read.

- Ask students to write short impressions, ads, or critiques. Exhibit students' work.

Students Prepare Book Reports

Writing book reports may be a tedious task. Better results may be achieved by using alternative formats.

Ideas for unconventional Book Report Activities

- Use audio or video equipment to record reactions to a book.
- Write a poem about the book or about an incident in it.
- Draw a picture that expresses some aspect of the book.
- Change something in the book. Personalize it; change an event, character, time, or place; or alter the ending.
- Design a new cover for the book.
- Design a record or a CD cover to accompany the book.
- Write a movie script or a play based on the book.
- Design a campaign to sell the book.
- Draw a cartoon that represents the book.
- Plan a debate about the book.
- Plan a TV presentation about the book.
- Make suggestions for changing the style of the book. For example, make it more romantic or comic or more like a science-fiction book.
- Pantomime an incident in the book.
- Write a newspaper critique. This activity works especially well with the classics. Ask students to pretend the book has just been published.

Chapter Two

▶ ▶

The Reading Comprehension Lesson: What is It?

Teaching reading is a complex undertaking. People have many different ideas on how best to approach it. No doubt, you already have some of your own. We would like, in this book, to share with you some ideas and procedures that you may find of value.

A reading comprehension lesson may use either a text-centered or strategy-centered approach. A text-centered lesson is dependent on the text selected, with the teacher emphasizing skills most appropriate for that specific text. A strategy-centered lesson, on the other hand, may focus on one or two strategies, using a variety of different texts. The ideas and activities presented in this book can be successfully applied to either type of approach to improving reading comprehension.

The reading lesson can be divided into three main components: pre-reading activities, while-reading activities, and post-reading activities.

PRE-READING ACTIVITIES

PRE READING Current research into the reading process demonstrates clearly that reading just because "the teacher said so" does not produce the proper expectations and pre-knowledge that are necessary for comprehension. A teacher should call on many important skills and strategies before actual reading begins. This practice induces a proper mindset, introduces the theme, activates previous knowledge, and motivates the learner to read the passage.

The sections that follow will present a selection of pre-reading activities. Choose the activity that furthers the purpose of the lesson.

PREDICTION

To establish the proper mindset and involve the reader in the text, use a prediction activity. Students may predict content by reading the title. They may predict genre (e.g., story, legend, newspaper article, scientific study) by noting format, illustrations, and charts. They may predict events by reading the first sentence of every paragraph. Chapter Five offers many prediction activities.

SKIMMING

Ask them to skim the passage for the gist. (Chapter Six will discuss skimming in detail.) This activity will allow students to develop realistic expectations about the actual content of the passage.

TEXT EXPLORATION

You may have your students explore the "universe of the text" (see Chapter Four). In many cases, information that is outside the text (information presented in photos or headings, for example) will familiarize students with the topic and the genre and thus prepare them for the reading.

ACTIVATION OF PRIOR KNOWLEDGE

To activate prior knowledge, ask your students questions that encourage thinking about the topic. Such questions may be used for group discussions, simulations or role-play activities. For example, for a lesson based on a text called "Improvements in Your Hometown," you might ask students, "What would happen if the government in our town decided to allot two million dollars to improving the town?"

A simulation activity based on the question could take place, with students choosing class members to act as mayor, residents, school principal, health officer, police officer, and so on. The students could conduct a simulated council meeting in which class members demand funds for various groups and try to reach a consensus about the allocation of funds.

Brainstorming is another way of activating prior knowledge. For a lesson designed to introduce "Improvements in Your Hometown," students could list as many of the new town's urgent needs as possible, each student selecting two or three needs that seem to be the most important and writing them on the board. The next step is to classify the ideas into appropriate categories.

WHILE-READING ACTIVITIES

WHILE READING In the text-centered approach, the selection of reading comprehension activities to enhance the acquisition of reading skills and strategies depends on the text you choose and on your students' needs. You will find an array of activities that are suitable for learners at different levels in this book.

Before deciding on while-reading activities, familiarize yourself with the text. What are its most salient features? Does it have a lot of new vocabulary? If so, go to the sections in this book that deal with lexical items (Chapters Three and Five). Is the reading a procedural text? If so, do activities designed to strengthen sequencing skills (see Chapter Seven). Does the text present cause-effect relationships? If so, do activities that deal with this type of logical relation. Is there much information that is not explicit? If so, do an activity about implicit information (see Chapter Five).

In other words, there is no optimal order for using the various activities in this book. There is also no ideal program that will suit the needs of all students at all times. Be flexible and creative in the choices you make. Your students should benefit the most by doing the activities that you think are most suitable for them.

Though while-reading activities activate processing strategies and encourage close reading, they also interrupt the reading process. Most while-reading activities can be done as post-reading activities, though the point at which the activities are introduced can change their purpose.

In this book you will find sample activities that deal with

- Making predictions while reading
- Revising predictions while reading
- Scanning for specific information
- Sequencing sentences or paragraphs
- Locating misplaced information
- Identifying the reasons and results in cause-effect relationships
- Noting text organization
- Locating markers that signal sequence, comparison, contrast, or cause-effect relationships
- Identifying the main ideas and supporting details of paragraphs or sections
- Locating examples that illustrate generalizations
- Identifying definitions
- Explaining or interpreting ideas
- Role-playing or discussing ideas or characters
- Recapitulating what the reader knows so far

POST-READING ACTIVITIES

POST READING After activating relevant skills and strategies during reading, learners are ready for other skills that are required of the good reader (see Chapter Eight). These are skills that encourage readers to go back to the text and to go beyond it.

In the Text

Some post-reading activities are designed to ensure that students understand the factual and explicit information presented in the text. You can strengthen factual comprehension by

- Asking questions that focus on who, what, where, why, and how
- Asking yes-or-no questions
- Filling in tables, charts, or graphs
- Matching pictures to text
- Matching text to text (e.g., sentence-completion exercises or matching causes and effects)
- Locating main ideas or supporting details
- Matching references to referents

Between the Lines

Post-reading activities can also ask students to make inferences and understand implicit information. You can activate students' involvement by

- Asking inference questions such as "What can we understand from . . . ?" or "What does this show. . . . ?"
- Looking at text from another point of view
- Continuing or concluding the text
- Matching implicit with explicit information

Beyond the Text

1. Transferring and integrating specific information to other contexts may include

- Role-playing or recreating sections of the text or the whole text

- Selecting items or ideas for further study
- Applying ideas, characters, or events from the text to a different setting
- Changing genre (e.g., from narrative to a newspaper report)

2. Text evaluation may encourage students to go beyond the text. To encourage students to evaluate what they have read, they may

- Distinguish facts from opinions
- Note bias
- Identify the author's point of view
- Identify and note connotations
- Perform a literary analysis

3. Consolidation and application activities may include

- Summarizing of main points and ideas
- Summary cloze activities
- Text mapping

SILENT READING VERSUS READING ALOUD

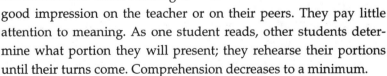

Reading aloud is a common practice in many language classes. This practice is important in that it allows a teacher to check pronunciation and reading fluency. Note, however, that reading aloud usually reduces comprehension. In most cases, students who read aloud are concerned with making a good impression on the teacher or on their peers. They pay little attention to meaning. As one student reads, other students determine what portion they will present; they rehearse their portions until their turns come. Comprehension decreases to a minimum.

Students' reading ability is often evaluated on the basis of their ability to read aloud. This is an unfortunate practice because the two skills should not be equated. Students may have very good pronunciation and mimicry abilities and yet not be able to comprehend what they read. On the other hand, students who have very good reading comprehension may—because of their personalities or lack of dramatic skill—dislike reading aloud and therefore perform poorly. Nonetheless, many students (particularly younger ones) enjoy reading aloud. They see it as an opportunity to perform in front of others. Do not discourage their desire to perform or deny them the opportunity to read aloud occasionally.

Some teachers have students read aloud to ensure that all students do the same thing at the same time. However, consider that the same reader reads different materials at a different speed, depending on circumstances (such as time of day) and the purpose of the reading (such as learning, answering questions, or reading for pleasure). Also consider that different readers read at different paces. Reading aloud or following another reader makes individuality in reading style impossible. Pace of reading is an acute problem for some FL/SL readers, and they should be given the chance to gain speed as they progress in their course of study.

By its nature, reading is a private, individual activity. Imagine someone reading the morning paper to you. It might be a frustrating experience to you. Reading for comprehension entails silence. This is a basic assumption in this book. Most of the reading activities suggested should come before or after a silent reading session.

SOME GENERAL COMMENTS AND SUGGESTIONS

As you prepare your lesson plans, keep these points in mind:

- ❱ Do not attempt to do too much in one lesson. Do not activate a variety of skills simultaneously. This may cause confusion.

- ❱ Reactivate skills already learned. Do not assume that skills activated in one text will transfer automatically to another.

- Make students aware of the purpose of the activity. This awareness may be valuable in itself and guide the learner in subsequent reading. You may, for example, close a reading lesson with an explanation like this: "In our reading lesson today, we looked at classifications for the purpose of recognizing ways in which writers organize their thoughts. For homework, look at other ways of classifying information."

- Any reading passage can be used to teach or demonstrate skills or strategies. There is usually no need to look for special texts.

- Do not expect your students to become proficient readers as a direct consequence of your explanations of reading skills and strategies. Good readers enjoy reading. They read regularly and read with comprehension. Provide your students with the proper tools, and you will help them along in the process of becoming proficient readers.

Chapter Three

▶ ▶

Dictionary Skills

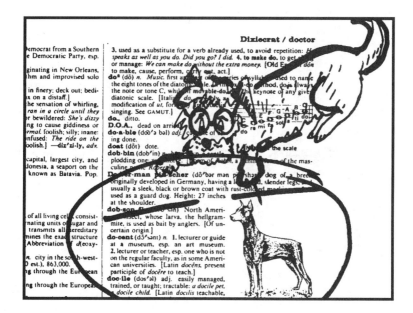

Dictionary skills enable readers to gain access to texts in a foreign language. For students whose native language uses the same writing system as the target language, specific instruction in alphabetization will be superfluous. However, alphabetizing and efficient use of dictionaries and reference materials in the target language are stumbling blocks for many language students.

Some students have access to electronic dictionaries, which allow them to type in a word and ask for its meaning. These students must still remember the order of the alphabet and be able to alphabetize so they can use nonelectronic reference materials that are organized in alphabetical order.

Encourage students to discuss the problems they have when they use a dictionary in a foreign language. The discussion itself will help alleviate some of their anxieties. In the discussion, you may want to

- Explain the difference between a *glossary* (which gives the meaning of a word in a specific context) and a *dictionary* (which provides all meanings). Have students prepare glossaries for people in different trades and hobbies, such as teachers, surfers, or astronauts.

- Consider the importance of guide words (the boldfaced words at the tops of dictionary pages), which allow fast, efficient use of the dictionary.

- Discuss phonetic transcription and its purpose in dictionaries. Although most students will probably not use the phonetic transcriptions at this stage, knowing what they are will make the dictionary less threatening.

- Introduce morphological concepts such as inflections (e.g., plural suffixes) and derivations (e.g., -*tion*).

- Stress the fact that synonyms usually have slightly different meanings. Absolute synonyms are rare. When two words originally have the same meaning, one or several developments usually take place: One of the words becomes obsolete (such as *thou*), one of the words changes its register and becomes more formal than the other (such as *seek* compared to *look*), one of the words starts to be used as part of a different set expression (consider the words *freedom* and *liberty*), or the words have different geographical or dialectal distributions (such as *elevator* and *lift*).

One activity to build dictionary skills involves learners in finding the exact meaning of each synonym. You might ask students to find the exact meanings and uses of words with similar meanings, *big* and *large*, for example, or *pretty* and *beautiful*. Or, you might ask students to consider connotations by looking up words such as *thin, slim, skinny,* and *gaunt.*

▶ Remind students that one word may have multiple meanings. To encourage precision, ask students to read the dictionary sample sentences listed under the various meanings of a certain word. The word *run,* for example, has more than 70 different meanings. The more frequently used a word is, the more meanings it acquires.

▶ Point out that the dictionary classifies a word according to its part of speech. Explain the common dictionary abbreviations for parts of speech and emphasize the importance of selecting the correct part of speech in looking up a word.

▶ Remind students that the dictionary can help them with their spelling. Point out how irregular verbs and the irregular plural of nouns are listed.

AWARENESS-RAISING ACTIVITIES

Discuss with your students the importance of locating a word quickly. Stress the following points:

▶ If they spend too much time locating a word, they may forget the context, what the word is, or why they are looking for it. Remembering the context is especially important since the meaning of a word can depend on it.

▶ If they spend too much time looking up words in the dictionary, they may eventually become bored and stop using the dictionary altogether.

Ask students to bring in alphabetically arranged books other than dictionaries—telephone directories, atlases, encyclopedias, and other indices. A short "looking-up" session may follow. Conduct this session at a fast pace.

ALPHABETIZING

The abilities to classify and alphabetize words are important for dictionary use. The activities that follow will help students practice these skills. Alphabetizing is particularly important to learners whose mother tongue uses an ideographic writing system such as Chinese.

 Classifying and Alphabetizing

1. Place each word in the appropriate column in the table.
2. Alphabetize the words in each column.

   apartment house, tiger, spaghetti, cards, cake, house, horse, sandwich, tennis, villa, summer, dog, pizza, chess, spring, turtle, fall, hockey, apple, lion, football, cat, castle, ice cream, winter, schoolhouse, basketball, museum

ANIMAL	FOOD	GAME	BUILDING	SEASON
				――
				――

The activity that follows provides practice in alphabetizing the second and third letters of words.

 Alphabetizing Words That Begin with the Same Letter

Here are some verbs. They all begin with the letter *t*.

turn, try, tie, travel, take, teach, tell, trust, throw, tear, talk, train, touch, think

Alphabetize the words.

To provide additional practice in alphabetizing, give each student a list that is partially alphabetized. Ask the students to find the words that are not in alphabetical order.

To provide a context, have students go back to a story they have read in class. Ask them to find words in certain groups, such as adjectives or past-tense verbs. Then have students alphabetize the words in each group.

Efficient Search Skills

Make students aware of guide words in the dictionary, and show them how these words facilitate a search. Ask them to provide guide words for a number of words they have to look up.

Speed Building

Have students bring in dictionaries. Most dictionaries can be divided into quarters.

1st quarter: A–D	*3rd quarter: M–R*
2nd quarter: E–L	*4th quarter: S–Z*

Use the concept of quarters to help students hunt for some words of your choice (preferably, familiar words). Have students work as quickly as possible. For example, you could ask the students to tell in which quarter of the dictionary they would find the words in the next two lists.

1. *January, February, March, April, June, July, August, September, October, November, December*

2. *banana, apple, pear, strawberry, berry, apricot*

If you wish, time the exercise to introduce an element of competition.

SCANNING

PRE READING Efficient use of a dictionary involves the ability to scan. To have students practice scanning, photocopy a page from the telephone directory. Ask students to scan the page for specific names, addresses, telephone numbers, and other information that you ask for.

WHILE READING You can also ask students to scan the dictionary to "disambiguate" homographs, words that are spelled similarly.

 SAMPLE ACTIVITY ## Using the Dictionary to Choose the Correct Spelling

Use the dictionary to decide which spelling is correct.

Dear Grandma,

*We are going to space. We're not going to **slip/sleep** at all. People don't need to sleep in space. **They're/Their/There** tied to their **sits/seats** all the time. They **seal/see** films about the earth. They don't have to **eat/it** in space. They can walk on the ceiling if they want to. We like that. Do you want to go **too/two**?*

Love,
The twins

AWARENESS OF COGNATES

Provide students with a list of words that pertain to science or technology (e.g., *archeology, anthropology, biology, compact disk, code, doctor, element, gas, geography, genes, pigment*).

These words have cognates in many languages. Let students translate the words into their native languages and tell the class whether the translated words are similar to or different from the target language words. Then ask each student to look up the words in the dictionary to see if their meanings and pronunciations are exactly the same in both languages. In most cases, the pronunciations will be different, but the target language word will be recognizable.

MULTIPLE MEANINGS

The following activities make students aware that the same word can have multiple meanings.

 Becoming Aware of Multiple Meanings

Read the text that follows.

COMPUTERS AND LANGUAGE

Can we use the computer to translate from one language to another? Many people think so, and they work very hard to make "automatic translating machines." Why do they have to work so hard?

We can put a bilingual dictionary into the computer memory. We can write a program that tells the computer to look at every word in one language and find the word in another language. Substitution is easy for the computer. So what is the problem?

---

 1. Pretend you are a computer and translate "Computers and Language" into your native language, one word at a time. Can you see why computer translation is difficult?[1]

2. Each of the following words has more than one meaning.
   fly, direction, program, grade, plan, product, passage

   a. Look up each word in a bilingual dictionary.

   b. Copy the meanings into the table. Note that the meaning of some words differs according to whether the word is used as a noun or a verb.

Nouns		Verbs	
English	Your Language	English	Your Language
fly		fly	
direction		—	—
grade		grade	
passage		—	—
plan		plan	
product		—	—
program		program	

   c. Can you see another reason why computer translation is not easy?

Chapter Four

▸ ▸

The Universe of Texts

Think of the information surrounding a text as the universe of the text. Such information includes titles, subtitles, the name of the author or authors, the date and place of publication, pictures and their captions, graphs, and tables. The audience (explicit or implicit) for whom the text is intended is also a significant element in the universe of the text.

Explore all these elements with your students. This chapter will present activities that will help you focus on several of them.

You may want to use a newspaper to help students become aware of the significance of elements that surround a text. Begin by identifying the physical features of a newspaper: the sections, headlines, subheadings, and columns. Note how print size, column width, placement on the page, and use of color and pictures affect the reader's perception of the importance of various articles.

Date of Publication

The date when a text was published can provide important information about the content of the text. If, for example, a reader knows that a text about architecture was written in the 18th century, he or she will expect the facts, ideas, and values presented in the text to be different from those in a recent text dealing with the same topic.

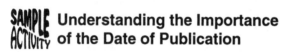 **Understanding the Importance of the Date of Publication**

The following text is taken from an encyclopedia published more than 50 years ago.

USEFUL GIANTS

Whales are the largest and the strangest of all mammals. They are very useful to people. The giant Blue whale and the Sperm whale are the most important for the whaling industry.

Whales are particularly important because of the valuable oils in the thick layers of fat under their skin. Whale oil is used as raw material for margarine and cooking fat. Whale oil has many uses in our great industries, especially in the manufacture of soap or cosmetics. One whale product, familiar to all, is liver oil, which is rich in vitamin A.

The hunting of whales has developed a lot since the times of the old sailing ships. Our modern whale hunting methods are efficient. Large numbers of whales are caught.

In the days of old whaling ships, sailors had a simple way of describing whales. They were called Wrong whales or Right whales. The Right whales were the ones that stayed on the surface of the water after being caught and could be brought to the ship easily. The Wrong whales were the ones that sank or disappeared from sight when killed. The Blue whale is a Wrong whale. If the harpoon can't hold it, it is lost.

During the days of the sailing ships, the hunting of Sperm whales was one of the most important activities in America. Oil from these whales was as important for lighting lamps in those days as gasoline is for running cars today.

Many things have changed since "Useful Giants" was written. Which sentences state true facts?

POST READING

1. Whales have become more useful.
2. Whales have become rare animals.
3. Whales have become less useful because we now have other kinds of oil.
4. Liver oil has been replaced by vitamins.
5. We have developed methods for keeping Wrong whales on the surface of the water.
6. Many great whales have been destroyed.
7. People have become aware that the destruction of whales may change the balance of nature.
8. Scientists have shown that whales are highly intelligent animals.
9. The public has become concerned with the future of whales.
10. The killing of whales has been greatly reduced.[2]

▶▶▶ INSIGHTS ◀◀◀

This activity makes students aware of the importance of paying attention to the date of publication. It is obvious that this particular article is outdated, and a lot of the views in it are no longer accepted.

Pictures and Illustrations

Pictures and illustrations often set the tone of a text. A text dealing with the environment accompanied by a peaceful scene or an illustration of flowers sets different expectations from one accompanied by a picture of a smoky chimney or a traffic jam.

SAMPLE ACTIVITY **Getting the Message from Pictures**

Read the following list of slogans.

Write the numbers of the pictures that might go with each slogan. You may use each slogan more than once.

1. Save the Environment

2. Stop Air Pollution

3. Protect Nature

4. Save the White Whale

5. Join an Environmental Organization

6. Cooperate to Save Nature

7. Stop the Development of Nuclear Power

8. Protect Marine Life

9. Fight the Killing of Kangaroos in Australia

10. Keep Rivers Clean

11. Don't Hunt

12. Stop the Needless Killing of Animals

13. Fight Acid Rain

14. Don't Use Animals for Research[4]

Graphs, Charts, and Tables

Graphs, charts, and tables usually add important information to the text. Reading the information in a chart or a table is a special skill that is usually dealt with in science and social science classes. The activity that follows will help the students integrate these skills into their general reading processes.

SAMPLE ACTIVITY Integrating Charts, Text, and Images

In this activity, you will learn about two friends, Ivan and Cynthia. The pie charts that follow show how Ivan and Cynthia usually spend their time.[5]

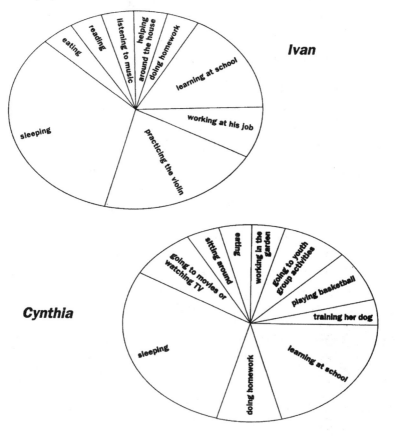

1. Ivan and Cynthia went on a trip. They wrote letters home.

   Which sentences come from Ivan's letters?
   Which sentences come from Cynthia's letters?

   a. Yesterday we went out to eat. I didn't have time to prac-
       tice, and I guess it was crazy to take my violin with me.
       Traveling isn't for me.

   b. I spent the afternoon skiing with John's friends. Skiing is a
       great sport. Good news. John plays basketball.

   c. Eating and driving around seem to be popular here. I'm
       getting bored and I can't wait to get home. I hate wasting
       my time like this.

   d. Yesterday I was on TV! I was invited to tell about youth
       groups and young people at home. Talking about home
       made me homesick.

   e. Yesterday Uncle Joe took me to the opera. I fell asleep!
       Listening to music just isn't for me! I felt very embarrassed.

   f. The best part of this trip is the new people I've met. When
       I get home, I think I'll join a youth group. Playing the violin
       is important, but music isn't the only thing in life.

   g. There are a lot of very poor people here. Seeing all these
       hungry people makes me feel lucky. I can work and earn
       some money. Here, even adults can't find jobs.

   h. I'm beginning to enjoy myself. I don't mind wasting time
       anymore. Yesterday we went to a drive-in movie and ate
       hamburgers after the movie. It's really hot here, so I guess
       we'll go to the beach tomorrow. I'm not bored anymore. I
       don't feel like listening to music.

   i. Seeing is believing! Yesterday I saw a girls' basketball
       team that was better than our girls' team back home.

   j. I taught John's dog a few tricks. Watching him look at me
       with his big brown eyes makes me miss Blackie. Is he
       OK?

2. Who do these belong to? Ivan or Cynthia?[6]

INTENDED AUDIENCE

Noting the intended audience is of great importance. Sometimes the audience is clearly defined. That is the case, for example, in texts which appear in specialized journals. At other times, the audience is a very general audience, such as that intended in texts in daily newspapers. In many cases, the audience has to be inferred by the reader. For example, a text about bridges published in a daily newspaper will be very different from one published in a journal for civil engineers or for architects.

Chapter Five

▶ ▶

Heuristic Processes

R eading is a process in which we constantly guess or make hypotheses and test them against the text. We bring to the text a knowledge of the world, of text types, of language structures, and of vocabulary. This knowledge is probably as important as the information we find in the text.

To see how the reader's knowledge enhances comprehension, read the following:

> **The princess ate some jam.**
> **The queen slapped her.**
> **The princess cried.**

According to Fillmore (Fillmore, 1981)[7] we read at different levels. While these sentences are disconnected, we read them on different levels, immediately imposing a family relationship on them and seeing them as a cohesive and complete text. We used our prior knowledge of princesses and queens to be able to do that. Our prior language knowledge now allows us to find a cause-effect relationship. That is, we envision some reason for the queen's slapping and the princess's crying. We even tend to impose an interpretation which is based on our personal knowledge and beliefs which go beyond the text. e.g., We assume that the princess was on a diet and was not supposed to eat jam, or that the princess was wearing a white dress and her mother was afraid she might get it dirty.

The following story will make the nature of prior knowledge clear. Stop after each sentence and ask yourself: Who is John? What makes you think so?

John was on his way to school last Monday.
(student? teacher?)

He was really worried about the math lesson.
(student? teacher?)

Last week he had been unable to control the class.
(math teacher? another teacher? parent?)

It was unfair of the teacher to leave him in charge.
(student?)

After all, it is not a normal part of a janitor's duties.

Try another experiment to help you appreciate the importance of prior knowledge. Read the text that follows.

> **It is structured as a series of modules laid in an increasingly common format: routines for which speed is not critical (initialization, instructions, etc.) are placed at the end of the listing, while routines that need to move along processing user input are placed near the top in priority order of need for speed.**

If you do not know anything about computers, the text probably did not make much sense to you, even though all the words and structures in it were familiar. The above examples show that:
- Background knowledge is often discipline- or culture specific.
- Implicit cultural knowledge aids understanding; the reader's response depends on cultural knowledge.
- Knowledge of vocabulary and syntax are less significant for comprehension than content knowledge.

Background knowledge determines what the reader expects from a text. These expectations allow the reader to use cognitive processes as tools to understanding. These processes include hypothesizing, deducing, predicting, and inferring and understanding implications. All these processes relate to guessing in one way or another and are sometimes referred to as heuristic processes.[8]

GUESSING WORD MEANINGS

This section will discuss several strategies for guessing word meanings: using context, guessing from morphology, using explicit in-text definitions, and being aware of restatements, examples, and explanations that appear in the text. The appendix contains a flowchart that suggests a procedure for teaching students about word meanings.

Encourage students to guess the meanings of words by making use of contextual clues. This is a skill most readers acquire naturally in their first language. When reading in a foreign language, readers may have to be taught techniques to enable the transfer of this knowledge to the foreign language.

Make sure students realize that it is not only the unfamiliar words that they need to clarify. Sometimes a new context can impose a completely new meaning on a familiar word. Discuss words with multiple meanings and ask the students to look up some familiar words that have unfamiliar meanings.

The purpose of the following activity is to show students how to cope with unfamiliar vocabulary using "nonsense words" which is how unfamiliar wrods appear to readers. The students should supply an actual word for each word in bold. Accept any word that makes sense. You might award points for supplying possible alternatives, thus turning the activity into a game.

Guessing the Meanings of Nonsense Words

The words that appear in **boldfaced** type in the following statements are nonsense words, but you can guess their meanings from the context. Write one or more real words that you could substitute for each nonsense word.

1. My father is a **bodder**. He can make beautiful things out of wood.
2. Alma is really **gribb**, but her sister is **gribber**, so she finds it easier to find jobs.
3. We decided to go for a **boorge** next week. However, if it continues to rain, we'll make other plans.
4. Have you ever visited **Ghordy**? In my opinion it's the most exciting place to visit.
5. Last night, both Sherry and David became very **gompered**. They wouldn't stop shouting at each other.
6. Anna decided to put on her new **shrusy** because she wanted to look nice for the visitors.
7. I think that show was **unbrindy**. I don't remember ever seeing anything so scary.
8. She told the story **shlaggily** because the ending is very sad.
9. He ran down the street very **brodingly** because he was late for his meeting.
10. Ben is quite **grappy**. He never lets anyone finish a sentence.

▶▶▶ INSIGHTS ◀◀◀

Most students enjoy the preceding activity. They are surprised to discover that many of their classmates inserted the same words they did. Explain that their ability to "understand" the nonsense words was based on background knowledge, their expectations of certain things happening in certain situations. Their background knowledge enabled them to guess the meanings of the nonsense words from their context.

The activity that follows will give students more practice at guessing meaning from context.

 ### Guessing the Meaning of a Word from its Context

The sentences that follow contain **boldfaced** words that may be unfamiliar to you. Each successive sentence presents a new clue about the meaning of the unfamiliar word. At what point did you guess the meaning of each word?

1. a. The entire village was **devastated**.
   b. The village was **devastated** by the invaders.
   c. The village was **devastated** by the invaders, and many people were killed.
2. a. Danny is an **industrious** student.
   b. Danny is an **industrious** student who does his homework every day.
   c. Danny is an **industrious** student who does his homework every day, works very hard, and enjoys it.
3. a. That's an **innovative** plan.
   b. That's an **innovative** plan that is really revolutionary.
   c. That's an **innovative** plan that is really revolutionary, and I'm sure it has never been done before.
4. a. She is a **competent** scientist.
   b. She is a **competent** scientist who well understands her work.
   c. She is a **competent** scientist who well understands her work. Her research is outstanding.

5.　a. He has to **reinforce** the foundation of his house.
　　b. He has to **reinforce** the foundation of his house, because one side of it is beginning to sink.
　　c. He has to **reinforce** the foundation of his house, because one side of it is beginning to sink. It is necessary to make it stronger immediately.

▶▶▶ INSIGHTS ◀◀◀

As a whole class activity, use an overhead projector to present one sentence at a time, demonstrating how context affects our comprehension as well as how clues can be gathered. If the students are doing the activity individually, have them mark the point (in each set of sentences) at which they feel sure that they have guessed the meaning of the marked word.

After completing the activity, discuss the implications with your students. It should be pointed out that the broader the context, the narrower the possible meanings of the word. If you feel that your class needs more guidance in doing the exercise, you can turn it into a multiple choice task, in which you provide possible meanings:

Devastated means: a. large, b. destroyed, c. built.

Your students will see that after reading sentence a, all three meanings are possible. After reading sentence b, meaning a is impossible. After reading sentence c, meaning b is clearly the only one possible.

 Increasing Your Awareness of Context

Can you guess what the **boldfaced** words mean? Choose the best option.

1. The rock singer was very popular. A **crowd** was waiting at the park to listen to her songs.
   Crowd means **lot of/a few** people.

2. Betty is a **curious** little girl. She always asks a lot of questions.
   A **curious** person **doesn't want/wants** to know many things.
3. There are many ships near our city, so there is a lot of **tar** in the water.
   When there is **tar** in the water, the water is **dirty/clean**.
4. I helped my friend in math. He was very **grateful**. He thanked me again and again.
   The word that helps us understand **grateful** is **friend/thanked**.
5. He ate **large amounts** of food, so he got very fat.
   Large amounts of food is **a little/a lot** of food.
6. I didn't **expect** a present from Danny, so I was surprised when he gave me a radio!
   To **expect** means to think something **is going/isn't going** to happen.
7. Sometimes we don't see things as they really are because our eyes can play tricks on us. These tricks are called optical **illusions**.
   An **illusion** is
   a. an unreal image
   b. a real image
8. They bothered me all the time. They had no **consideration** for my privacy or my need to rest.
   To have **consideration** means
   a. not to care about other people's feelings
   b. to care about other people's feelings
9. I was probably the wildest little kid in our neighborhood. By the time I was five, I had fallen out of a tree, cut my sister's hair off, and gotten lost twice. My mother said I was **mischievous**.
   A **mischievous** child is a child who
   a. can cause harm in the course of playing
   b. always behaves well

10. "Excuse me," said the girl. "I thought you were somebody else." She was very **embarrassed**.

When you are **embarrassed**, you feel

a. proud

b. uncomfortable

c. satisfied [9]

This activity demonstrates how context can be used to clarify meaning. It is important to encourage students to utilize the context before they refer to the dictionary to look up the meaning of words. They may then find that using the dictionary is actually unnecessary in many cases.

USING MORPHOLOGY TO GUESS THE MEANING OF WORDS

Point out that in many languages words can be broken down into three basic parts: base word, or root; prefix; and suffix. Familiarity with common base words, prefixes, and suffixes can help students guess the meanings of unfamiliar words. You can help students become familiar with common affixes by presenting words in families, as the next activity does.

SAMPLE ACTIVITY   Breaking up Words to Guess Their Meanings

Try and guess the meaning of each word in each group by breaking the words into their component parts.

1. **change:** changeable, changeful, changeless, unchangeable, changeability, changeover

    honor: honorable, honorably, dishonor, honorary, honorific, honorless, dishonorable

    interest: disinterest, disinterested, uninterested, interested, interesting, interestingly

2. Write the meaning of each prefix in the list that follows.
   pre-, pro-, re-, un-, anti-, auto-, co-, in-, mis-, dis-, un-, in-, con-, en-, de-

Write two words that use each prefix.

3. Write the meaning of each suffix.
   nouns: -er, -or, -ist
   adjectives: -able, -ful, -less, -ing
   nouns: -ment, -ship, -ness
   adverbs: -ward, -ly

Write two words that use each suffix.[10]

4. Use the prefixes and suffixes in the preceding activities to build words from the base words that follow. See how many you can build.

   like, port, press, tract, nature, kind, joy, port, limit, quiet

USING DEFINITIONS TO UNDERSTAND WORD MEANING

 Definitions Provide Easy Access to New Vocabulary

Look at the following sentences. Find the definition and the word that is being defined. Do you understand what the word means?

1. Camouflage, or protective coloring, helps an animal hide.
2. Motivation—that is, the willingness to act—is the secret to a successful career.
3. A motorbike, sometimes called a motor scooter, is an important means of transportation in many countries.
4. Literacy, defined as the ability to read with understanding, is a concern for most educators.
5. Mountaineering, the sport of climbing mountains, is a very popular sport in many countries.
6. He is mostly concerned with the formation and origin of the Earth; in other words, he is a geologist.

7. A skyscraper, which is a tall building, dominates its surroundings.

8. A space station—a kind of platform floating in space—will be used in the future as a meeting place for space vehicles.

Restatements, Examples, and Explanations

In the following examples, pay attention to the way restatements, examples, and explanations help you understand the meaning of the boldface word.

1. A **sledge** is used to carry people and goods in the snow.

2. He is a **loner**; he invites no one and keeps his address a secret.

3. To build the new club, they **pooled their resources**, each giving a small sum of money.

4. She likes warm colors such as red, scarlet, and **vermilion**.

5. This knife is so **blunt** that it does not cut at all.

6. The story was so **moving** that everybody cried.

7. Everyone can vote in our country: the educated and the ignorant, the **affluent** and the poor. [11]

▶▶▶ INSIGHTS ◀◀◀

The techniques that allowed you to guess word meaning in these sentences are varied. In sentences 1 and 5 guessing meaning is possible because the sentences explain or imply how the object the boldfaced word represents is used. In sentence 2, the restatement of the idea of "loner" allows you to guess the meaning of the word. Restatement is used in sentence 3 as well. In sentence 4, a series of examples allows you to guess the meaning of the word "vermilion." In sentence 6, you can infer meaning through consequences. In sentence 7, contrast allows you to guess meaning.

Cloze Techniques for Guessing Word Meanings

A closed cloze activity, where the options are provided, may be used to encourage attention to context. Students have to choose the best word for each blank. This requirement encourages guessing a word from the context.

Read the following passage and choose a suitable word from the list for each blank. There are more words than you need. You may use the same word more than once. Use the glossary or your dictionary to help you.

admiration, case, crime, cruel, expect, innocent, law, powerful, problem, punished, rewarded, solution, trial, weak

---

SOLVING A CASE

Detective stories are very popular. We read them, we see them in the movies, we watch them on television. In many cases we guess the ending long before the book or movie is over. How do we do that? What makes us predict so well? Why do we [1]_____ things to happen as they do? Is the story similar to real life? Well, very few of us live a life of [2]_____. We don't break the [3]_____. For most of us, the detective story is not like real life. So why are our predictions usually right?

Our predictions are usually correct because all detective stories are similar to one another. There are "good guys" and "bad guys." The bad guy is [4]_____. He commits a crime. The good guy is accused of a crime, but we know he is [5]_____.

The wrong person is accused. We know the truth. We want to tell the good guys, but we can't. We aren't in the story!

The good guys are weak, and the bad guys are [6]_____. They commit another [7]_____. Another innocent person suffers, but the truth will finally come out. The criminal will be [8]_____. The innocent person will be [9]_____.

The guilty person will be brought to [10]_____. The brilliant detective will present his solution of the [11]_____. Everyone will be full of [12]_____ for the detective.

We knew the solution all along![12]

In this activity the guessing technique is reversed. Instead of guessing the word from its context, students have to choose the most suitable word for the context. This reversal provides variety of formats and helps students focus on constructing meaning into a text.

PREDICTION

Prediction is an important strategy both in the pre-reading and the while-reading stages. Before we begin to read a text, we usually have a good idea of what the text is about, and sometimes we even know what it will include.

Think of how we read a newspaper. When we read the heading of a report, we already know a lot about it if we are familiar with the topic. We use headlines to build certain expectations about the contents or tone of the article. Our expectations may be wrong, but we use them to prepare ourselves for what is to come. If we continue to read for details, we have a general idea of what to expect. We continue to make predictions as we go along. We predict the next word in the sentence; we predict the idea following. If the paper is taken away from us, we will be able, in most cases, to say what the next word and the next idea were. We can do it because of our "predictive abilities."

In other words, we predict on the basis of our prior knowledge. This knowledge is the basis on which we acquire new knowledge. When reading, we always predict. We become aware of our predictions only when we are wrong. When we recognize that we have made a mistake, we usually have to reread a word, a sentence, or a section. When our expectations are met, we are not aware of our predictions. We just go on.

A valuable experience is to stop our reading from time to time, to assess the "predictive ability" we have.

Consciousness-Raising Activity

Discuss with your students the importance of prediction in reading in any language, and emphasize how making conscious use of this strategy when reading in a foreign language can help us understand a text. One possible way of illustrating the importance of predicting is to ask students for examples of how we use prediction in our everyday life, and then, by extension, in reading. For example, when the phone rings, we "guess" who it might be and prepare our reactions in our minds; when we take a test, we "predict" our grade and usually "come prepared" to receive it. We are not aware of these predictions, but in most cases we can tell that we predicted because there is no "surprise" involved. It is only when we are surprised (How come this person called? How come I got this grade?) that we realize our predictions went wrong.

Introductory Activity

This is a simple activity that can be used in class to introduce the concept of prediction.

SAMPLE ACTIVITY

1. "Be careful with this knife," mother said. "It can be dangerous. You can cut your hand if you aren't careful." "Sure, sure," Eric said. He really wasn't listening. He was looking at his sister decorating the cake. He thought that he would like to taste the icing.

WHAT WILL HAPPEN NEXT?
  a. Eric will have an accident.
  b. Eric will taste the icing.
  c. Mother will get angry.

2. "I heard that they're hiring students down at the cafeteria," Mr. Jackson told his son. "Perhaps you can find a job there." "Yes," Ron answered, "But I heard that you have to pass a physical test for the job." His father said, "You're healthy! Why don't you try it?"

WHAT WILL HAPPEN NEXT?
  a. Ron will take physical fitness lessons.
  b. Ron will apply for the job.
  c. Ron will not apply for the job.

 ►►► INSIGHTS ◄◄◄

In this activity students are only exposed to the first stage in the process. Because the prediction questions are not followed by a reading passage, students do not get a chance to check or confirm their predictions.

As a follow up activity, have students write a continuation based on their predictions and justify the course they chose to take. They will learn that in prediction one may refer to "good" or "fair" guesses, but one cannot judge answers as right or wrong before the rest of the text is read. This realization should encourage students who are concerned about making mistakes to try to predict.

USING CONNECTORS TO PREDICT

One way of enhancing the students' ability to predict information is to acquaint them with logical connectors (such as **but, however, nevertheless,** etc.). Most connectors prepare the reader for the information that follows and thus facilitate anticipation.

Distribute a handout with incomplete sentences to your students. Ask each student to complete the sentences. Compare endings. Take a vote! Your students will be surprised to find out how similar their endings are.

 Focussing on Logical Connectors

Complete the following sentences.

1. We took an umbrella because _____
2. He decided to postpone his holiday because _____
3. When he heard the news, he _____
4. His salary is low; however, _____
5. You may watch television now. However, _____
6. Take out a pen and a piece of paper in order to _____
7. Take off your shoes because _____
8. She was born in Paris, but at the age of 20 _____
9. She used to ride a bicycle, but now _____
10. Her mother approved of her plans. However, _____

▶▶▶ INSIGHTS ◀◀◀

In this activity, a very limited context (half a sentence) is provided. The possible predictions are also limited. The advantage of focusing on connectives is that the general direction in which the writer's thoughts will proceed is immediately clear. Even at this low level, students are made aware of the heavy semantic weight that these words may carry.

PREDICTING AS A PRE-READING ACTIVITY

Associating as pre-reading

You can use mapping as a pre-reading activity for an expository text. Begin with a central topic word in the text. Put it in the middle of the board. Have students brainstorm around this word. Then, add their ideas around the word. You may get something like this:

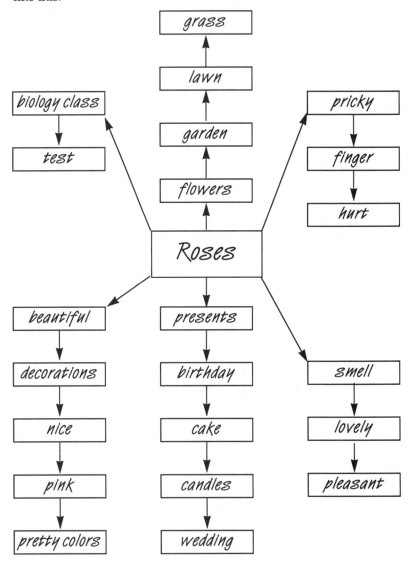

In most cases these associations can facilitate reading because they constitute topic-relevant predictions.

PREDICTION BASED ON PRIOR KNOWLEDGE

The activity that follows shows how making predictions based on prior knowledge can enhance the comprehension of a text.

 Making Predictions Based on What You Know

What you know about a subject may help you understand new information you read.

 You are going to read an article about turtles.

Do you think the following facts are correct? Write **Yes** or **No**.

1. ___Turtles live only on land.

2. ___They are almost blind.

3. ___They eat animals and plants.

4. ___They can live more than 100 years.

5. ___They "sleep" all winter.

6. ___They have live babies.

7. ___They have four legs.

8. ___They can't hear very well.

9. ___They can weigh up to 400 kilos.

10. ___They are found only in hot regions.[13]

TURTLES

Turtles are reptiles. They have 4 legs, 2 lungs, and hard shells. Their mouths are similar to birds' beaks, and they have no teeth. They "sleep" during the winter. They sometimes live for more than 180 years! They have good sight but poor hearing. They can make sounds.

The smallest turtles are 4 inches or about 10 centimeters long. The largest turtles weigh about 850 pounds or 400 kilos and can be as long as 3 yards or 3 meters. Turtles are found in most parts of the world, but many turtles live in the tropics. Turtles can go without food for a long time. Once a year the female lays her eggs on land, usually in a hole she digs with her legs. Turtles eat little plants or animals.

Baby turtles know what to do as soon as they are born. They can walk and swim right away. They know what to eat and where to find their food. They know when to hide in their shells, and when it is safe to come out again. So, the mother turtle doesn't have to feed, teach or protect her young turtles.[14]

 POST READING Go back to the questions before the text. How many answers were confirmed?

PREDICTION THROUGH BRAINSTORMING

Brainstorming is a highly successful activity for expository texts.

Write the title of the text on the board (e.g. Growing Roses, Black Holes, Raising a Pet).

Students write
- ▶ two facts that they already know about the topic
- ▶ two things that they don't know about the topic.

> two things that they want to know about the topic.

You may conduct the whole activity on the board or on a large poster. Students may sign their names next to each entry. At the end of the lesson you may return to the entries made, and acknowledge those students who predicted the most, and those whose questions were answered.

Predicting from the Title

Predicting some of the content from the title is a strategy most good readers use automatically. This anticipation helps them decide if the text is likely to interest them, if they need or want to continue reading it or not. To help students develop this habit, use questions like those in the following activity. They focus the learner's attention on key words and concepts in the title, and on the logic of the message.

 Read the title of the following text.
1. What do you know about dolphins and tuna?
2. Are dolphins related to tuna?
3. How can the fishing of tuna become a threat to dolphins?

TUNA FISHING THREATENS DOLPHINS

Since 1959, about 3,500,000 dolphins have been killed as a result of tuna fishing. For reasons not yet understood, large groups of tuna are often found swimming under large groups of dolphins. Fishermen follow and chase the dolphins, and then they set nets around them. They often throw bombs from helicopters into the groups of dolphins. This practice cuts their tuna fishing time in half.

Until the 1950s tuna were caught one by one. Even then, fishermen knew that tuna and dolphins often swam together, and they often used the dolphins to find tuna.

Nowadays, however, circular nets which are over a kilometer long are set around entire groups of dolphins. The nets are closed at the bottom, trapping both the dolphins and the tuna. Because dolphins are air-breathing mammals, they drown when trapped in the nets.

In 1972, the US government passed a law which limited the number of dolphins that could be killed by US tuna ships. New dolphin-saving fishing techniques were developed. Dolphin deaths from US tuna fishing activities, once over 200,000, were reduced to about 20,000 per year—a 90% reduction. But it seems that the only way to end this killing is to outlaw the capture of dolphins during tuna fishing. Only then can we be sure that the tuna that we buy does not mean the death of over 130,000 dolphins per year.[15]

PREDICTION FROM HEADLINES

Cut up newspaper headlines and distribute them at random to groups of 4 or 5 students. Groups should try to guess as much as they can about the content of the article. They should also note any related vocabulary items they expect to find in the article. When they are done, provide the original articles and let students note differences and similarities between the original and their predictions.

PREDICTION BASED ON CONTENT WORDS

The following prediction activities prepare the reader for the stories that follow. There are no right or wrong answers at the pre-reading stage. Encourage students to discuss their answers and to explain the reasons for their decisions. By making intelligent guesses, they will establish a framework for understanding the story. The class can try to guess the plot outline of the story that they are about to read. They may later compare this outline to the actual story line. Questions after the story encourage a confirmation of the students' predictions.

The words below appear in the following story:

professional, cups, trophies, fast, potential, coach school hero, basketball player, game, pressure, team, gym, running, shape, sport, medals, tryout, track

Predict:
1. What is the following story about?
2. Where is the story going to take place?
3. What do you think is going to happen?

RUN FOR YOUR FUTURE

Everyone knows what I am going to be. I'm in the Gordon family, aren't I? Bob Gordon, my Dad, was a famous basketball player—a real professional. Dan Gordon, my oldest brother, played all through high school and won his team the cup of the year. John Gordon, my other brother, got a basketball scholarship to college. Who knows where he'll stop? The kids in school still remember Tommy. He's only three years older than I am. Tommy was last year's hero. He has at least eight trophies at home. And now, it's my turn. I'm tall—just like the other Gordon boys. I'm fast, really fast. Everyone knows that I'm the next basketball hero—maybe even with professional potential. Dad talked about my first season all through dinner last night. It's only the second day of school, and Coach Kim is already looking at me in the hall.

Here I am. His next school hero. That's it. We're the Gordon brothers—basketball players. But the game makes me nervous! I can't stand the coach pushing me. I hate the pressure of the team. When we lose, one thousand disappointed eyes watch me leave the gym. When I get home, one of my brothers always has some advice to give me. The truth is—I don't like playing basketball.

What I like is running. When I run, the world opens up for me. I test my power. I am a king. I spend a lot of time running. My dad can understand that. "It keeps you in good shape for the game, Son," he says, and he gives me a manly pat on the shoulder. Dad can't understand that running is a sport. Many times I've wanted to say, "Listen, Dad. I'm not going to be a basketball player. I hate basketball. I'm going to be a runner. I'll win medals. You'll be proud of me even if I don't play basketball."

Jimmy Gordon was sitting on the bench in his school gym. He was thinking. His friend Alex was sitting beside him. Jimmy wanted to tell Alex how he felt, but he didn't want to talk about himself. Tryouts for the basketball team were about to begin. This was the moment to decide. Alex was looking down at his shoes. "Jimmy," he said. "You're a great runner. Really great." Jimmy looked up surprised. "What are you trying to say?" Alex didn't answer right away. "O.K. sport," he finally said. "Show the coach what you can do."

Coach Kim was standing in front of Jimmy. "Jimmy," he said, "you don't have to try out. You're on the team. Any member of the Gordon family is on my team."

Jimmy looked at him and smiled. "I have a little brother," he said. "He's pretty good."

"What are you talking about?" Coach Kim asked.

"I can run," Jimmy said. "I'll be a great runner someday. Do you want to be my coach?"

Before Coach Kim could answer, Jimmy left the gym. He left the school building. "How am I going to tell Dad?" he thought. Then he began to run around the school track. He ran like someone who could get to the Olympics. He ran so fast that he felt like a bird flying. When he finally stopped, he sat down on the grass. His mind was empty. When he looked up, he saw Coach Kim. The coach was looking at him. There was a smile in his eyes.[16]

 POST READING Read your answers to the questions on page 59. Were you right?

You Are Going to Read a Story About a Magic Show.

1. Read the list of words in the table. Look up the words you don't understand in your dictionary.

2. Which of these words do you think you will find in the story?

	I'm sure it's in the story	Maybe it's in the story	I don't think it's in the story
a stick			
the ocean			
a crowd			
friendship			
excited			
a stage			
jealous			
to forgive			
shopping			
strange			
curtain			
to bow			
a counter			
to applaud			
mysterious			
a trick			
to pour			
to burn			
a cloth			
empty			
decisions			
to steal			
a hall			
shy			
an audience			
a seat			
a theater			
a rabbit			
a sleeve			

17

Notice that these activities are valuable vocabulary activities. Students will need to know the meaning of the words to be able to make sound predictions. Words used as distractors may be taken from the following text, or from previous texts. This format may be used for prediction with any story. Note also that at this stage students have a fair amount of knowledge about the story, and they are motivated to find out more.

USING CONTEXTUAL CLUES

Misleading Clues - Guessing in Riddles

In riddles, the fun depends on people's wrong guesses. In stories (unless they belong to the genre of "surprise ending" stories) and articles, however, readers are expected to make correct and intelligent guesses as they go along, and various clues or signposts (lexical, grammatical and contextual clues) in the text will guide them along.

 Two Riddles

1. A man built a house all by himself. He worked very hard for many months, and in the end he finished his work. When he finished, he had one brick left. What did he do with it?

Answer: He threw it away, of course!!

2. Once upon a time, a little old lady who loved dogs put all of her puppies in a basket and got on a train. In her cabin sat a man who was smoking a cigar. The little old lady couldn't stand the smoke and politely asked the man to put out his cigar, but he wouldn't. After a while she asked him once again, but again he refused, so she decided to take matters into her own hands. She got up, grabbed his cigar and threw it out the window. The man got very upset and in revenge grabbed one of the puppies and

threw it out the window. The little old lady rang the alarm, and the train stopped. They got off and saw the puppy running towards the train. It had something in its mouth. What was it?

Answer: It had the brick in its mouth!!

►►► INSIGHTS ◄◄◄

Most readers will probably give another answer. Most probably their answer to the second question will be "the cigar." Why did they make the wrong guess? Because they were deliberately misled.

Readers should pay attention to those clues when reading. When reading in a foreign language it is particularly important that they do so, as this "predictability" in a text will help them understand the flow of thought.

Leading and Misleading Clues in Narrative

The following activity illustrates the importance of awareness of clues that lead or mislead the reader.

This story is based on true events that happened to real people.

READING TO GRANDPA
by Ed Aloris

I was probably the wildest little kid in our neighborhood. By the time I was five, I had fallen out of a tree, cut my sister's hair off, and gotten lost twice. The only one who had any influence on me was my grandfather. When I was with him, I felt calm and grown up. He lived in another city, but I always went to visit him on holidays.

Grandpa was tall and had big blue eyes. He was really strong looking, and I was always proud to walk with him. He had a beautiful walking stick, and he looked like a king. He had a way of making me feel the world. He would say, "It's cool," and we would look up to the sky as the cool wind brushed our faces. I would look at the clouds and see them for the first time. He taught me to identify the calls of different birds. Even now I listen to the sounds of nature in the special way he taught me.

Grandpa liked to be read to. Everyone read to him. Mother would read to him for hours. My aunt and my uncle had their turn on weekdays. At times, even my father took a turn and read to him. My grandfather would listen carefully, and from time to time he would ask a question. All this seemed very natural to me.

I always knew that one day I would also read to Grandpa, but I had to learn how to read first. Once I could read, I would have my turn and would become a member of the adult world. I wanted to learn quickly. Reading to Grandpa meant being grown-up. It was more important than riding a bike or playing ball.

Everyone was very worried about how I would manage in school. I remember my father saying, "How will that little devil sit on a chair for an entire day?" My teacher was a hard woman. She had a very serious face. She always wore a dark high-necked dress and brown walking shoes. There were many children in our class. We sat in double rows on small wooden chairs. We sat straight with our hands folded behind our backs. We hardly moved. We were afraid to speak. Most of the time we read out loud. I remember sitting very quietly, trying to be very good and paying careful attention to the reading. That's all I remember myself doing. My report card was excellent, and my parents were very proud. "Well, well," my father said, nodding his head in approval.

That summer's visit to Grandpa was very special. I carefully packed my book in my little suitcase. At the last moment, just before we left the house, I checked to make sure the book was still there. It was. Well, I was ready to go.

On the way, I couldn't stop talking. I was going to read to Grandpa! Mother seemed excited too. "Grandpa will be really pleased," she said. It made me feel adult and important. When we arrived, she said, "Dad, guess who's going to read to you today?"

Grandpa smiled. "Well, I think I can guess. He's a big boy now." He was sitting in a huge velvet armchair. I sat down on a stool beside him.

I read to my grandfather all afternoon. I read the whole book to him, from cover to cover. Everybody was serious and quiet. I read in a loud, strong voice. My mother was smiling the whole time.

I was the center of attention. Even my father listened to me for some time. Grandma served her special cakes and drinks, but I was too busy to eat or drink. I went on reading. Everyone congratulated me. It was a wonderful day. I had finally done it. "You see," my mother said. "He may be mischievous, but it's because he's clever. All clever children are mischievous."

The following afternoon Grandpa gave me a blue book that had a picture on the cover. "Today I want you to read this book to me," he said. "You'll like it. It is very interesting." He smiled. "But, Grandpa," I said. "I don't know this book." Grandpa smiled. "Just read," he said. "I know you can."

All the fun was gone. I was in a panic. I looked at the book for a long time. Grandpa sat silently, bending over his walking stick, waiting. I looked at him. I looked at his eyes. Nothing. There was no expression in them. He was just waiting patiently. For the first time, I realized that he was not looking at me. He was sitting, his back straight and firm, and he wasn't looking at anything. His big blue eyes were staring into space.

I tried to read. I tried hard, but the letters made no sense. The words were strange. There were so many on the page. I looked at the second page. There was a picture. I told Grandpa about the picture, and he listened carefully while I described it. He asked a few questions. He wanted to know about the colors in the picture. I described all the colors, and I felt much better.

"This is a very pretty picture," Grandpa said, "I like it very much. It sounds very interesting. Now, read." I tried again. I looked at the words, but I didn't know what to do. I didn't know this book. Suddenly, I saw one word that was familiar. "Yes," I said. "Here is a word I know. Dog." "Dog," I read out proudly. "Very nice, thank you very much," Grandpa said. I knew something was wrong, and I felt as if I couldn't breathe.

Mother walked in. "Well," she asked. "How is it going?" Grandpa was very serious. He asked me to go out and play. Mother sat down beside him. I walked towards the door very slowly. As I was walking out, I heard Grandpa say, "Don't you understand? The child can't read. He learned his whole school book by heart." What did Grandpa mean? Hadn't I read him an entire book? I remember feeling very sad. I sat on the steps in front of the house, and I decided that I would never read again.

Mother called me back into the house. Everyone was smiling again. I was puzzled. Mother said very cheerfully, "Grandpa likes your reading very much. You will go on reading to Grandpa for the rest of the summer." I felt confused. "Yes," Grandpa said, "You will go on telling me about the pictures and reading me stories, and maybe someday you will write your own stories, and other people will read them."

It was only much later that I understood that my grandfather was blind. None of the people around me, neither my family nor my teacher had seen that I had a reading problem. Only Grandpa saw and understood. He was the only one who really listened to me. He didn't need eyes to see.

To this day, I don't understand how Grandpa managed to teach me how to read. But by the end of that summer I was reading well. Grandpa had not only taught me how to read, he had taught me to love books.

There are many clues in this story. They are meant to lead the reader to the truth. However, there are sentences in the story that are meant to mislead the reader. These sentences lead the reader in the wrong direction.

1. Classify the following sentences.
    a - clues that the boy couldn't really read.
    b - clues that the grandfather couldn't really see.
    c - sentences that mislead you.

1. He had a beautiful walking stick.

2. We would look up to the sky as the cool wind brushed our faces.

3. Grandpa liked to be read to. Everyone read to him.

4. My report card was excellent, and my parents were very proud.

5. I read the whole book to him, from cover to cover.

6. "But, Grandpa," I said. "I don't know this book."

7. All the fun was gone. I was in a panic.

8. I looked at his eyes. Nothing. There was no expression in them.

9. For the first time, I realized that he was not looking at me.

10. He was sitting, his back straight and firm, and he wasn't looking at anything.

11. I tried to read. I tried hard, but the letters made no sense. The words were strange. There were so many on the page.

12. He wanted to know about the colors in the picture.

13. "This is a very pretty picture," Grandpa said. "It sounds very interesting."

14. "Yes," I said, "here is a word I know. Dog. Dog." I read out proudly.[18]

Prediction through Selected Contextual Information

 Suppose you are going to read a story. Before you read it, read the following:

There are two important characters in the story:

▶ A magician

▶ A man in the audience, called "the Quick Man."

Here are some of the things the characters in this story say:

The magician: "I will now present to you the famous Japanese Trick."
"Will some gentleman kindly let me use his hat?"
"Will you let me smash your glasses with my hammer?"

The Quick Man: "He-had-it-up-his-sleeve."
"He probably had some more rings."
"I don't understand this at all."

Try to predict.

1. What is going to happen in the story?
   Write three sentences.

2. What will the magician do to the Quick Man?
   Write a sentence.

3. What will the Quick Man do to the magician?
   Write a sentence.

Decide who each sentence is about.

M = magician **Q** = Quick Man **A** = audience

1. He took a bowl of goldfish from an empty cloth.
2. He said to the people near him, "He-had-it-up-his-sleeve."
3. They whispered around the hall, "He-had-it-up-his-sleeve."
4. He frowned.
5. He took seventeen eggs from a hat.
6. He went on whispering as the magician performed more tricks.
7. He threw a watch on the floor and took a hammer from the table.
8. He put a hat on the floor and jumped on it.
9. He was fascinated by the real mystery.
10. He was beginning to look puzzled.[19]

▶▶▶ INSIGHTS ◀◀◀

In this case, we do not provide the students with the story. However, by now, they have a good idea of the story line, the events that took place and the developments in it. If they feel they want to read the story, it means that the activity:

▶ Produced a good set induction

▶ Motivated them to read

▶ Made them curious

▶ Provided the proper mood

▶ Introduced the main characters and ideas in the story

When using the following suggested activities, you may wish to put a text on a transparency or on a handout. If you put it on a handout, you can cut the various sections of the text and give them to your students "in bits." The class can work in pairs or in groups. Only when a group has finished answering the questions on a section do they get the next section.

Prediction in Narrative

The following is an example of a narrative and the types of questions that can be used while reading (the questions are in bold letters).

A TRUE STORY

On a gray morning in the spring of 1988, a boat circled slowly near Quebec, Canada. Those on board the boat were looking up at a high cliff.

1. Why were they looking up?

Two climbers on ropes were battling to open a large banner. The banner snapped above them in the wind. Everyone was nervous.

2. Why were they nervous?

Loose rocks were falling off near the climbers. The climbers were hanging several hundred meters up. They were in real danger. The people on the boat barely breathed. They realized that their friends were climbing on a cliff that was badly cracked. The banner that the climbers were holding was flying in the wind and hitting against the cliffs. Every time the banner hit the cliff, more rock broke off.

3. What kind of banner were they holding?

They were trying to save nature. And yet, for a moment it seemed that nature was their enemy.

4. What kind of banner were they holding?

Would they succeed or would the wild winds overcome them? The climbers slowly and carefully climbed down the mountain. Finally, the sign could be seen. It said: SAVE THE BELUGAS.

5. What or who are the belugas?

6. Why should they be saved?

The belugas are white whales. They live in northern rivers and oceans. Once they lived in the waters of Western Europe, but they cannot live there any more. They are also disappearing from Canadian waters because of water pollution.

Pictures of these men climbing the huge rock were seen by millions of people all over the world. Many people heard of the belugas for the first time. More people became aware of the danger whales are in.[20]

▶▶▶ INSIGHTS ◀◀◀

Notice that not all the answers contain the same degree of prediction or imply the same reading processes. Questions 1 and 3 may produce a variety of predictions based on the students' social and cultural background, without much help from the text. Questions 2 and 4 demand inferencing and can be partially answered on the basis of the information gathered from the text. The last two questions can be answered even by students who never heard of the belugas, by making intelligent inferences from the text. They may not know the facts about the belugas, but they may be able to conclude that they are endangered animals that are environmentally important.

Prediction in an Expository Text

The following are examples of expository texts that can be used in class to practice the important skill of prediction. They are broken up at intersections which most clearly demonstrate signposts used by readers to predict. Use the same procedures as in the previous activity.

The first text in this series illustrates a controversy. The concept itself should be discussed to help students predict in the "right" direction.

SHOULD WE WORRY ABOUT GLOBAL WARMING? A SCIENTIFIC CONTROVERSY

1. What do you think the passage is about?
   Why do you think so?

Most scientists agree that there will be some global warming. However,

2. How do you think the sentence will continue?
   Read on and check your guess.

not all scientists agree about the effects of global warming. For example, some scientists predict that New York City and other coastal cities will eventually be covered by the ocean. Others

3. How do you think the sentence will continue?
   Read on and check your guess.

believe that coastal cities are not in any danger. They don't know exactly what changes will take place or when they will take place.

4. What do you expect to read in the next paragraph?
   What makes you think so?

Scientists also disagree about how much global warming can be expected. Some think that global warming may be only half as great as predicted.

5. How does the next sentence begin? Write the first word, then read on to check your guess.

Others predict that we are heading towards a climatic disaster if the greenhouse gases increase by 1%.

The big fear of environmentalists is that the planet will grow so warm that

6. How will this sentence end?
life will be almost impossible. However,

7. What do you think will come now?

a number of scientists have developed theories that lead to more optimistic predictions.

8. Were your expectations met?[21]

▶▶▶ INSIGHTS ◀◀◀

Notice that there are a number of skills involved here. Question 1 is for predicting from the title and subtitle, which capitalize on students' previous knowledge in two areas: global warming and the concept of what a controversy is. Thinking about these allows learners to make sound predictions about content and possibly the organization of the text: argument -> counter-argument -> conclusion. Questions 2, 3, 5, 6, and 7 are based on the learners' familiarity with logical markers and possible logical relations. For example, they know that **however** marks a contrasting idea, and **therefore** may predict the following words quite accurately. Or, they may predict the idea expressed by the word "others."

Making Predictions in Expository Text

The text that follows will be interrupted by questions that will help you make predictions about what you are reading. Write the letter of the prediction that most closely matches your own.

HOW MONEY DEVELOPED

Long ago, no one needed money. People grew their own food or hunted it. They made their own clothing and shelter. As time went on, some persons found that they could do certain jobs better than their neighbors. They began to spend their time doing those jobs. They then exchanged the things they produced for other things they needed but did not make themselves.

What kind of information do you expect to get now?
   a. What happened as time went on.
   b. What people do now.

A man who liked to fish and was a good fisherman spent his time fishing. He traded some of the fish he caught for spears, clothing, and other items that his neighbors made. This method of trading or exchanging goods is called barter. Barter works well when people do not need or use a wide variety of goods. Primitive tribes in various regions still use barter.

People often had problems in using the barter system.

What do you expect now?
   a. examples of problems in using the barter system
   b. an explanation of the barter system.

For example, a man who raised sheep might find that the only person who wanted a sheep was a fisherman. Suppose the shepherd traded one sheep for a hundred fish. He would then have to exchange the fish that he could not eat before they spoiled. Frequently, he could not find people who would accept the fish in trade for other goods he needed. And so he lost the value of the unused fish.

As time went on, people began to use metal money more than any other kind of exchange because it was more practical.

What kind of information do you expect now?
    a. disadvantages of metal objects
    b. other advantages of metal objects
    c. a new topic

Metal objects did not wear out easily. They also had a wide range of values depending on their weight, and they could be broken into smaller pieces.

Historians believe that the Chinese may have used specially shaped metal money as early as 1100 B.C. This money consisted of miniature bronze spades, knives, and other tools. The tool-shaped money represented the objects that commonly were exchanged in barter.

▶▶▶ INSIGHTS ◀◀◀

The basic principle involved here is that when readers make hypotheses about what they are going to read and then check their hypotheses against the text, they become more deeply involved in the reading process and can therefore achieve a better comprehension of the text. It is a good idea to have students go on reading after each question to check whether their predictions were confirmed.

INFERENCE AND IMPLICIT INFORMATION

In any reading, some of the information must be supplied by the reader. If all the information were explicit, most of the things we read would be long and boring. Writers rely on the intelligence of the reader to supply some of the information from their general world knowledge and to infer some of the information from the text itself.

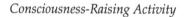

Consciousness-Raising Activity

To make students aware of the distinction between explicit and implicit information, the class can be asked to interpret a number of pictures:

First, the students are asked to describe what they see in the picture (i.e., the explicit information in it). Then they are required to explain what their interpretation is (i.e., the implicit information they gather). For example, in a picture of a man sitting by a window and looking out, the students will first describe exactly what they see. Then, they will interpret the picture basing their interpretation on the explicit information. One student might say that the man is tired, so he decided to sit by the window to relax a bit after a day's work. She will probably use some of the details in the picture to justify her interpretation. Another might think that the man is sad because of something that happened that day, so he decided to be by himself for a while. She will probably point to the man's facial expression or body posture.

The purpose of such an activity is to increase students' awareness of the two different types of information one can gather from any given piece, either written or pictorial.

Introductory Activities

The following is used to demonstrate implicit information in daily experiences and show learners, explicitly, how they can easily recover the message that is conveyed. You may use this activity for class or individual work.

SAMPLE ACTIVITY

SIGNS

Information

Sign	Explicit	Implicit
1. Wet paint	The paint is wet.	Don't touch! You may get dirty!
2. Reserved	Someone reserved this seat.	You can't sit here.
3. Stop!	Don't move.	Danger ahead.
4. Quiet!	Don't make noise.	This is a hospital or a library.
5. Inflammable	This can burn.	Don't light a fire near this.
6. Sale	Things are sold here.	Prices are lower than usual.

Ask students to add other items to the table.

Ask learners to cut out advertisements from newspapers or bring pictures of traffic signs and/or posters in their immediate environment to class. Then assign pair work. Students are to study the ad, sign, or poster. Student A will write a summary of the explicit information in it (e.g. Stop! Drink X!) while student B summarizes the implicit information such as "Danger ahead!" "Pay attention!" "Look in all directions!" "When you drink X, you feel cool, young, pretty, healthy," etc. The second step is to exchange roles, student A doing the implicit information and student B the explicit information. The third stage is to compare their summaries.

SAMPLE ACTIVITY — Understanding Non-Verbal Messages

Answer the questions about each picture.
Discuss the meaning of each message.

1. What is the dog trying to "tell" us?

2. What is the dog trying to "say"? What should you do?

3. What does this sign mean? What should drivers do?

4. What does this sign mean? What should drivers do?

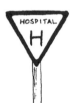

5. What does this sign mean? What should you do when you see it?

6. What do you have to do?

7. What do drivers have to do? Why?

8. What does this picture mean? Can you think of other ways to express a similar meaning?

9. What does this gesture mean?

10. What is the dog trying to "tell" us? What could you do to help it?

11. What does this person feel?

12. What is this person "saying?"

13. What is this person trying to "tell" us? Where could she be?

14. What do these pictures mean? Which of these pictures gives more information? Which picture do you prefer?

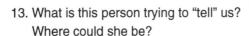

22

This activity is based on inferencing from pictorial material that is mostly symbolic in nature. The nature of symbols and how they are used to convey simple messages may be discussed. This is an appropriate time to introduce pictorial symbols that your students are not familiar with in their own culture and to compare symbols that they may know about in other countries.

MAKING INFERENCES FROM LISTS OR TIME LINES

 Important Steps in the Development of Mass Communications

The questions in this activity will ask you to make inferences based on the explicit information in the list that follows.

1.	105	The Chinese made paper and ink.
2.	900-1450	Book scribes became very skillful.
3.	1456	The Gutenberg Bible (the first printed book).
4.	1450-1550	Printing developed all over Europe.
5.	1621	First news sheet in Amsterdam.
6.	1638	First printing press in America.
7.	1665	First English newspaper, "London Gazette."
8.	1690	First American newspaper, "Public Occurrences," Boston.
9.	1702	First daily newspaper in English, "The Daily Courant," London.
10.	1731	First magazine, "The Gentleman's Magazine," London.
11.	1833	First inexpensive newspaper: "The New York Sun." Very popular.
12.	1844	Morse sent first telegraph message.
13.	1853	Paper made from wood.
14.	1867	First easy-to-use typewriter.
15.	1876	Bell sent the first telephone message.
16.	1877	Edison invented the phonograph.

17.	**1894**	First film.
18.	**1895**	Marconi sent and received radio messages.
19.	**1906**	Human voice was heard on radio.
20.	**1923**	First picture televised between New York and Philadelphia.
21.	**1928**	First Walt Disney animated cartoon.
22.	**1941**	First commercial television programs.
23.	**1954**	Beginning of color television programs.
24.	**1972**	First video recorder.
25.	**1979**	First fiber-optic cable.

Write the answers to these questions.

1. What did people read before the first newspaper was printed?
2. Were there book scribes before the year 900?
3. Were there typewriters before 1867? If so, what was wrong with them?
4. Which came first: printing or writing?
5. Before 1833, were newspapers cheap or expensive?
6. Before 1833, did most people read newspapers? [23]

▶▶▶ INSIGHTS ◀◀◀

The nature of the information in this activity–short, self-contained facts–makes it possible to close-read the explicit information quickly. At the word level, words such as: **first, inexpensive,** or **beginning,** facilitate inferencing. Students apply logic to the information provided in order to derive additional information.

Inferencing Activities Based on Short Texts

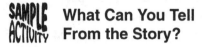 **What Can You Tell From the Story?**

1. When people talk about treasure, they often think of money, silver, or gold. There is another kind of treasure. We see it when we go to museums. It is what we know of our past. Museums are important because they keep treasure where everyone can see it.

From the text we can infer that the writer believes that history is ...

2. The teacher left us alone the other day. She had to go to the office. Everybody started to play. Dan threw an eraser at Sara. "Stop that," Sara asked. "Ha! ha!" He laughed. Just then Mrs. Ferguson opened the door. She asked angrily, "What's going on here?"

From the story we can infer that Mrs. Ferguson is the...

3. "Come into my office," said the principal to Mark. "You know you must come to class on time. If this happens again, I will have to expel you."

From the story we can infer that Mark ...

Inferences from a Text

 **Strange Habits!!**

Report 0079......To: Planet 7XZ@ From: Planet Earth

Dear Friends,

Life here is very strange. The earth people look a lot like us, except their eyes aren't purple. Their head is full of long thin strings, which they call hair. They aren't very tall. They eat animals and vegetables. Can you believe it?! They grow something they call fruit. It is the only thing I can eat, and I am always hungry.

Most of them can't stand on their heads, so they don't fill up their batteries. They close their eyes!!! At night they lie down in soft beds for at least 6 hours. Some of them spend more than 8 hours in bed. 15-year-olds sometimes stay in bed for 12 hours!

They speak a very simple language. They call it English. I understand them quite well. They don't understand our language, so I speak to them in English. They ask me a lot of questions, and they are happy to tell me about themselves.

I am staying with a very nice young man. His name is Marty. He calls me Spacey. Marty has an animal in the house. This animal is small, eats special food, and barks at night. Marty goes to work every day. The people here work for money. They need money for everything they do. When Marty goes to work, I use the time to think and to write my messages to you.

Tonight I am going to a party. The earth people make loud noises and they jump around at parties. I think that they have a lot of fun. They have many strange habits, but I hope to understand them better soon.

Until my next report, I am S P A C E Y

 POST READING Marty asked Spacey a lot of questions. Here are some of them.

Do you know the answers?
1. Do people speak many languages on Planet 7XZ@?
2. Do you eat meat?
3. Do you have computers on your planet?
4. Do people speak English on your planet?
5. Do people on your planet have pets?

6. Do they listen to music?
7. Do you dance?
8. Do you sleep in a bed?
9. Do you use money?
10. What do you eat at home?
11. Why do you stand on your head every night?
12. How do you fill your batteries?
13. What do the people on your planet look like?
14. What is the name of your planet?[24]

▶ ▶ ▶ INSIGHTS ◀ ◀ ◀

Notice that the questions are inference questions. The answers are not in the text, they are "between the lines." To answer question 4 as **no**, students must be able to infer that people on Spacey's planet don't speak English because if English were used on that planet, there wouldn't be a need for Spacey to describe English to his friends.

The next activity is based on the text "Tuna Fishing Threatens Dolphins" on page 57.

 POST READING After students have read the text, have them answer the following questions:

1. We can understand that before 1959
    a. methods for catching tuna were old-fashioned.
    b. few dolphins were killed as a result of tuna fishing.

2. We can understand that before 1959
    a. dolphins guided fishermen to tuna.
    b. people didn't know that tuna and dolphins often swam together.

3. We can understand that
    a. it is easier to find dolphins than tuna.
    b. it is difficult to find tuna because they hide under dolphins.

4. We can understand that when fishermen follow dolphins, they hope to
     a. catch many dolphins.
     b. find tuna as well.

5. Circular nets for catching tuna were developed
     a. in the early 1960s.
     b. in ancient times.

6. Dolphins die in the nets because
     a. they can't breathe.
     b. they are brought to shore.

7. New dolphin saving fishing techniques were developed in the US.
     a. as a result of the 1972 law.
     b. because there was less demand for tuna.

8. The number of dolphins killed every year is about
     a. 200,000.
     b. 20,000.
     c. 130,000. [25]

In the next activity students distinguish material that can be inferred from material that may be true but is not mentioned in the text. There is room for interpretation here, and therefore students may differ in their answers. They should be told that different answers may be acceptable if they can justify their decisions.

 Old "Facts"

Until the 16th century, everybody believed that the world was flat. People believed it was a real fact. People never walked upside down, so the world had to be flat! When brave sailors sailed to distant places, they had to be ready to face a terrible danger: falling off the earth! Columbus proved that it was possible to reach the east by sailing west.

Until the 19th century, everybody was sure that there was a "fire substance" inside a match. They thought that all things that could burn had "phlogiston" in them. They believed that "phlogiston" was a chemical element that caused burning. Today we know that "phlogiston" doesn't exist. But ask a young child where the fire is before you light a match. He or she will tell you that the fire is inside the match. The young child doesn't know about oxygen. People before the 19th century didn't know about oxygen either.

New discoveries change what we believe to be true. They change the facts because we understand what we see in a new way. Today there is so much new information in the world that it is very difficult to know all the facts about anything. Even while you are learning, someone in the world is probably adding new knowledge that isn't in your books. In ten years, some of the things you are learning right now will be outdated!

POST READING

When we read, we can understand many things. Some of them are not in the text, but we "read between the lines." We can infer them. Other things are not in the text and not between the lines.

Decide	Between the lines	Not in the text at all
1. Scientific knowledge never changes.		
2. Knowledge is based on facts and opinions.		
3. Columbus was very brave.		
4. People believed in phlogiston because they were uneducated.		
5. It is not important to study any more because things change all the time.		
6. We need to know the facts to be able to understand change.		

26

The following activity illustrates a different format that can be used to encourage inferencing. It activates the inferencing of reasons and conclusions from a narrative. It is based on the story "Run for Your Future" on Page 59.

Complete these sentences for Jimmy.

There are several possible answers.

1. Everyone knows what I am going to be because_____.

2. It's only the second day of school, and Coach Kim is already looking at me in the hall because_____.

3. I hate the pressure of the team because_____.

4. What I like is running, but_____.

5. Dad can't understand that running is a sport, so_____.

6. Many times I've wanted to say, "Listen, Dad. I'm not going to be a basketball player, but_____."

7. "You're a great runner. Really great." Alex said to me.
   I was surprised because_____.

8. "I'm going to be a great runner someday. Do you want to be my coach?" I left the gym before Coach Kim could answer because_____.

9. The coach was looking at me. There was a smile in his eyes because_____. [27]

It is important to encourage diversity of answers in such an activity. The logical connectors **but** and **because** affect the meaning of the sentences and guide the students' inferences. However, they do not dictate a single possible answer.

EXPLICIT AND IMPLICIT INFORMATION IN TEXTS

The following are two possible activities based on the same text.

a. Give each student a copy of the entire text as presented below. For each piece of implicit information listed, have students find the explicit statement in the text which is the source of this information.

b. Give students a copy of the text only (6 paragraphs). In groups, have the students list as much implicit information as they can elicit from each paragraph. Do the first paragraph with them to show them how much implicit information is taken for granted and how each implicit statement has its source in an explicit phrase from the text. Compare the students' lists with the ones given.

 Bees' Built-In Clocks

Dr. August Forel, a Swiss scientist, noticed in 1906 that bees are excellent timekeepers. He used to eat breakfast on the terrace at the same time every day. He noticed that bees always seemed to be buzzing around, trying to get a taste of the jam.

Implicit information:
- Before 1906 no one paid attention to this phenomenon.
- The weather was very agreeable in Dr. Forel's place of residence.
- Dr. Forel was a punctual person.
- Bees like sweet foods such as jam.

Dr. Forel got interested in the behavior of bees. He checked the terrace on mornings when he ate inside. The bees were there. This puzzled him. Was it the smell of fruit in the jam that attracted them? If so, how could they know what time to come when there was no jam out there?

Implicit Information:
- ▶ Dr. Forel looked for the bees on mornings when he ate inside.
- ▶ Dr. Forel was puzzled by the fact that the bees kept coming when there was no jam.
- ▶ The bees came at the same time every day.
- ▶ Bees must have some "built-in" clock.
- ▶ This "clock" must have told the bees when to come.

Karl von Frisch decided to study the behavior of bees, and in 1940 he designed an experiment to find out if they had an inner clock.

Implicit Information:
- ▶ By 1940, scientists had an idea about the inner clocks of bees.
- ▶ Although many years had passed between the first time scientists got interested in this quality of bees (1906) and the studies of von Frisch (1940), the actual facts were not yet known.

Karl von Frisch built a box to hold the bees and decided to put them on a fast boat to the United States. Would they keep feeding at German local time? Or would they shift their feeding time as they crossed time zones?

Implicit Information:
- ▶ Karl von Frisch lived in Germany at the time.
- ▶ If the bees continue feeding at German local time that would mean that they had internal clocks.
- ▶ If the bees shift their feeding time, that would mean that they respond to some external clue.

Karl von Frisch got a student to take the voyage with the bees. He waited patiently for the reports. However, the student had been seasick the entire time and was never able to get out of bed.

Implicit Information:
- ▶ The student did not write any report.
- ▶ The reports were supposed to have indicated the bees' feeding times.
- ▶ The experiment failed because of the student's seasickness.

In June, 1955 Dr. von Frisch and Max Renner designed another experiment. In Paris, Renner trained bees to come to a feeding dish between 8:15 and 10:15 in the morning. When they were well trained, he packed them in a box and flew with them to New York. In less than 24 hours they were in the Natural History Museum in New York. At 3:15 in the afternoon, local New York time, the bees came out of the hive to feed.

Implicit Information:
- ▶ Fifteen years passed between the first experiment (1940) and the second (1955).
- ▶ The second experiment was much more effective, as this time there were fast transatlantic flights, and there was no danger of seasickness.
- ▶ The whole experiment lasted exactly 24 hours.
- ▶ The experiment gave an answer to the question raised by Dr. Forel about 50 years earlier (1906).
- ▶ The conclusion of the experiment was that bees do have internal clocks.
- ▶ The internal clock of bees does not seem to be affected by external conditions, such as weather conditions or geographical location.

Chapter Six

▶ ▶

Processes of Analysis

In his Rhetoric, Aristotle speaks about "topoi" or ways of thinking about a topic. Thinking about the topic is one of the most important ways of beginning to analyze a text. One looks at the information in the text, at the logical relationships in it and at the hierarchy of ideas. The most prominent ones are recognized as main ideas.

In order to read with comprehension, readers must analyze the information presented and classify items or ideas into meaningful units. We make associations of words and ideas that have something in common, and we also compare and contrast them. In other words, we discriminate among words and ideas and look for similarities or differences so as to make sense of the text.

In summary, when analyzing, we recognize examples and illustrations, definitions and factual information. That is, we learn to focus on the salient information presented and pay less attention to information that is less important or redundant.

LOCATING MAIN IDEAS

Understanding texts depends on understanding the most important ideas in them. Main ideas usually appear in typical locations.

Various procedures of textual analysis show regularities in the organizational structure of texts. Different genres have different organizational patterns. Awareness of these patterns facilitates text analysis and comprehension.

Narrative texts, like stories or accounts of events, display clear categorization based on setting, events, episodes, reactions, resolutions, responses, and their relation to each other. These texts seldom create problems for the student. Expository texts, which present theories, ideas, or facts, are organized along content and structural elements such as rhetorical organization, patterns of argument development, and categories of ideas.

In order to read expository texts with comprehension, readers must be able to recognize the theme, to analyze the information presented, and to classify items or ideas into meaningful units. This ability is not always acquired naturally, particularly when reading in a foreign language.

Associations of ideas and words that have something in common are made by using a variety of cognitive strategies. To read expository texts with comprehension, readers often need to be taught to focus on the salient information presented and to pay less attention to information that is either peripheral or redundant.

The recognition of main ideas implies the recognition of subordinate organizational categories such as classifications, comparisons and contrasts, definitions, and examples. All these help the student locate the important information or main idea by distinguishing it from the supporting material.

It also implies the recognition of a variety of markers whose function is to highlight the information they precede. These markers focus the reader's attention on what the writer considers important. It is crucial that students become familiar with those signposts in a text, as foreign language learners tend to cling to what they understand, thus imposing an artificial hierarchy on the text.

A variety of discourse markers indicate that what follows is worthy of special emphasis. These markers do not always emphasize the main idea, but it is worthwhile paying attention to them so as to see what it is the writer considers important.

Discourse Markers that Signal Main Ideas

important to note, most of all, a significant fact (factor), a primary concern, the most substantial problem, a key issue, the main feature, especially, most noteworthy, remember that, a major event, the chief issue / outcome / feature, the principal item / thought / idea, pay particular attention to, the chief factor, a vital problem / issue / factor, above all, a central..., a distinctive..., especially relevant, must / should be noted.

The conventional location of main ideas in many expository texts is either at the beginning of the paragraph (deductive pattern) or at the end of the paragraph (inductive pattern). This conventional location aids readers in identifying the important concepts. Their identification precedes their comprehension but does not necessarily imply it.

PRE READING ## Skimming

This skill is important as a pre-reading activity. By skimming a passage before reading it, especially when reading expository texts, readers get an overview of the whole text, its contents and organization. Skimming also allows us to locate the main ideas quickly. This skill should be explained and practiced.

To skim means to look through a passage **quickly** in order to see what it is about. When you skim, you don't read every word. You usually look at the beginning of each paragraph.

1. Skim the passage "Hobbies" quickly.

Find the paragraph that each of the following items describes. Write the letter of the paragraph in the space provided. One is done as an example.

_____ Hobbies that require time
_____ Hobbies that both children and adults have
_____ Hobbies that cost a lot of money
__A__ Hobbies in the past
_____ Why are hobbies a good thing?
_____ Hobbies for one or more people
_____ What are hobbies?

2. Skim the same passage again and find the following:

1. a very old hobby:_____
2. a hobby that requires a lot of time:_____
3. a hobby that both children and adults like:_____
4. an expensive hobby:_____
5. something people collect:_____

HOBBIES

A   During the Middle Ages, only the rich could have hobbies. The poor didn't have any free time. Nowadays, it is possible for almost everyone to have a hobby. In fact, hobbies are more popular nowadays than they were in the past.

B   Hobbies are activities that people like to do in their leisure time. They take people away from every day routines. They help people relax. They entertain and give pleasure. Many hobbies are many centuries old—music, dance, poetry, drawing, painting, sculpture, doll-making, raising pets, making jewelry, and magic are some examples.

C There are many kinds of hobbies. Some require quite a lot of time. For example, if you collect stamps, you need time to organize them and put them in albums. If your hobby is dancing, you probably spend a lot of time practicing.

D Some hobbies are favorites of children and adults alike. For instance, both children and adults like to collect things. They collect many kinds of things. Both young and old people collect coins, dolls, stamps, paper napkins, matchboxes, stationery, paintings, autographs, postcards, maps, buttons, bottles, records, plane tickets, posters, rocks, sea-shells, and butterflies.

E Some hobbies are quite expensive. If your hobby is airplane modeling, you will need to spend money on materials. If it is painting, you will have to buy paints, brushes, and special paper.

F Some hobbies, such as reading, are for you to do when you are alone. Others, like sports, are social hobbies.

G Hobbies provide entertainment and pleasure. For that reason, when you work at a hobby, you don't usually get very tired. You do something you enjoy doing, and time passes quickly![28]

In the following activities, the learners have to match rules with explanations, or headings with passages. They concentrate on the contents of the reading passage or explanation and choose the main ideas expressed in a condensed form in the title or rule.

SAMPLE ACTIVITY Categorizing: Choosing a Suitable Label

1. **Look at the table.** Choose suitable titles from the following list. Then copy them at the top of each column. You have more titles than you need.

   Type, Characteristics, Animal, Limbs, Home, Name, Species, Qualities

bear	mammal	4 legs	cave	big, hairy, sleeps through the winter, good parent
bee	insect	6 legs & wings	hive	makes honey
camel	mammal	4 legs	desert	humped back, long neck, stores fat, can go two weeks without water
cat	mammal	4 legs	homes & farms	color-blind, purrs, eats mice, domesticated
chicken	bird	2 legs & wings	farm	can't fly high
cow	mammal	4 legs	farm	raised for its milk
dog	mammal	4 legs	homes & farms	intelligent, color-blind, domesticated, good sense of smell

29

▶ ▶ ▶ INSIGHTS ◀ ◀ ◀

In this activity students need to find a suitable superordinate word that includes the examples given. Note that the superordinate word (animal, limbs, etc) constitutes a generalization of the information in that column.

SAMPLE
ACTIVITY **Matching Rules
and Reasons**

Match the rules and the explanations by writing the number of the
rule in front of the right explanation. Remember that the explanation
must be logically related to the rule.

When Vegetables are Cooked

Vegetables provide minerals and vitamins, but many of these are
lost when the vegetables are prepared and cooked. Here are some
rules that will help us save the vitamins and minerals in vegetables.

1. Vegetables must be washed quickly.
2. They should not be peeled or cut up.
3. They should be boiled in as little water as possible.
4. They should be cooked for a short time.
5. Vegetables must be cooked in covered pans.

___ The skins of vegetables have most of their minerals.
___ By standing in the water, vegetables lose their minerals.
___ When vegetables are boiled in a lot of water, the minerals and
some of the vitamins dissolve in the water.
___ Air destroys some of the vitamins.
___ Heat destroys some of the vitamins.

What to Do in Case of Fire

The following are some rules that you should follow if you see a fire.
Read the explanations and match each one of them with the suitable rule.

1. Report the fire at once to the fire department.
2. Clear away from the fire any material that will burn.
3. Cool the burning material so it is no longer hot enough to
burn.
4. Don't pour water on blazing oil.

5. Use water, sand, or dirt to put out small fires.

6. If your clothes catch fire, don't run.

7. Lie down on a blanket or coat and roll yourself up in it.

___ This action will shut off the supply of oxygen and your clothes won't continue burning.

___ You should know what phone number to call. If you don't know, ask the telephone operator.

___ By throwing water on the fire, one can put the fire out.

___ This action would bring more oxygen to the burning clothes and make them burn faster.

___ This action shuts off the supply of oxygen. Without oxygen, the fire can't burn.

___ Fat is lighter than water, so it floats on top of the water.

___ If you do this, you will keep the fire from spreading. The fire usually cannot jump across a clear area.

▶▶▶ INSIGHTS ◀◀◀

Note that the rule is the concept or idea that lies behind the explanation. Activities 1 and 2 alert students' previous knowledge schemata. If there are any gaps in the knowledge schemata, matching rules to explanations should make them explicit. Students will understand the consequences, that purposes and reasons are related to each other, and that conditions are related to results.

 ## Matching Scrambled Paragraphs with Suitable Headings

The Industrial Revolution in England

The list that follows presents the results of the Industrial Revolution:

1. There was less need to do things by hand.

2. People could do more work because they used the power of wind and water.

> 3. Many new machines were invented.
>
> 4. The problem of placing the new machines was solved.

The paragraphs that follow describe the changes involved in the Industrial Revolution. For each lettered item, write the number of the result that the changes caused. You will refer to only three results.

a. An invention called the steam engine gave people a new supply of power to do work. The engine used heated water, which turned to steam. Steam pressure supplied the power the people needed.

b. During the 1700s, people in England invented new machines that were different from those that had been used before. These could do many jobs that had previously been done by hand.

c. Most of the new machines were so large and needed so much power that workers could not put them in their homes. Instead, special buildings called factories were built. Workers were hired to come to the factories to run the new machines.

To extend the preceding activity, ask your students to suggest a suitable title for a text made of the paragraphs labeled "a" through "c." If students suggest illogical titles, discuss why the titles are unsuitable.

Examples of suitable titles:

Important Changes in England

The Beginning of the Industrial Revolution

The Development of the Modern Factory

Examples of unsuitable titles:

How Steam Power Changed Our Lives (Steam power did indeed affect the way we live today, but the title is unsuitable because the paragraphs do not discuss the relationship between steam power and modern life.)

The Industrial Revolution in the United States (This title is unsuitable because the text discussed England, not the United States.)

Energy Problems (This title is unsuitable because the text discussed factors in addition to the problem of getting enough power.)

 **INSIGHTS**

Suggesting suitable titles requires students to make inferences about a whole text rather than just a paragraph and to seek a clear theme that is common to all the paragraphs in the text. Discussion of possible titles will lead students to realize that people interpret the same text differently. To extend the activity further, ask students to try to convince others that a particular title is better than the others.

HEADLINES AS MAIN IDEAS

A headline prepares the reader for the article to come. It must be short and to the point and contain the main idea or state the topic of the text. Newspaper headlines generally make excellent examples of concise statements of the main idea of a text. To show your students how a headline reflects main ideas, separate the headings from newspaper articles. Distribute articles and headings randomly. Students should move around the room to find "their" article. They should ask each other questions about content, until they are sure they have found the article for which they have a headline.

Read the following passage and then complete the table of contrast with the "main" information about the three types of societies discussed.

Family Patterns

Many societies have been organized according to the so-called "familistic" or great family pattern. Whole communities or villages were made up of relatives, with the oldest man in charge. Typical of the great family pattern have been the families of China, Poland, and Russia.

The great family is under the authority of the elders. Very old customs and traditions determine the great family's way of life and its values. The individual's will is subordinate to the family's.

In contrast to the great family is the small family pattern that is typical of most parts of the United States. This family, instead of being familistic, is individualistic. Instead of the elders controlling affairs, each individual couple makes its own decisions. Husband and wife and their children alone are the family unit.

The small family pattern differs from the great family in another important way. In the great family, custom, tradition, and the rule of elders relieve young people of the responsibility for making decisions. In the small family a young person may choose his own course. This means that the small family allows the individual greater responsibility.

Another type of family, which falls between these two types, is the stem family. The authority of parents, typical of the familistic pattern, prevails here too. The birth rate is high, but many children go away from home and become individualistic. One or more of the children remain at home and take over as soon as the older generation dies. Stem families are common in parts of western Europe and isolated rural areas of the United States. The mountaineer family is typical.

Type of family			
Size			
Authority (decision making)			
Factors influencing decisions			
Example			

Use the information in the table to express the main idea of the passage in no more than two or three sentences.

Compare your statement of the main idea with your friends'. Did you choose to include the same elements? Did you organize the information similarly? What were the reasons? Discuss.

▶▶▶ INSIGHTS ◀◀◀

This activity demands that students focus on the prominent information about each type of family so as to comprehend the differences among them. In the passage the main ideas are clearly stated and the organization of the paragraphs is conventional. Moreover, the inner organization of all paragraphs is similar.

By transferring the information from the passage to the table, students discriminate, select, and summarize the content.

Note: The marker "another important way" in paragraph 4 illustrated the fact that markers of prominence are not always followed by the focal elements in the text.

POST READING Using Main Ideas to Organize a Flow Chart

Read the following passage, and then transfer the relevant information to the chart.

Compare your chart with your friends'. Discuss differences.

WHAT IS COMMUNICATION?

The word *communication* comes from Greek: *communis*-common. In order to communicate, you need two or more persons. To have communication, you must have some kind of message. Both the sender and the receiver must understand the message. If someone speaks to you in a foreign language, the message will be more difficult to understand.

People communicate in many ways. Messages can be spoken, written or visual. We can show happiness by speaking, writing, smiling or making gestures. The deaf use sign language to express themselves. The sign language of the deaf is made up of standard signs. People that are not deaf also use signs to express themselves, but these signs are not standard.

Can you understand someone without saying a word? Can you look at someone and know what she is feeling? Can you send a message to someone by just looking into her eyes and thinking your message? Can you manage through a day without using your voice? If you can do these things, it doesn't mean that you can read thoughts, and it doesn't mean that you are telepathic. It probably means that you have good facial expressions and clear gestures. You are also good at reading other people's expressions and gestures.

Small children are usually excellent at understanding gestures. They learn to understand spoken language by watching other people. They even learn the meanings of words and sentences by understanding the movements that are used with the sentences.

We can understand English or any other foreign language better if we watch the person we are talking to. For this reason, when people are speaking in a foreign language, it is more difficult to understand them over the phone. Better communication takes place when there is eye contact.

We actually see much more about what other people are communicating than we realize. We can learn to pay attention to the smallest changes in people's expressions and become better at using and understanding nonverbal communication. The more we understand what people are saying to us, the more we will be able to guess what they aren't saying.

SAMPLE FLOWCHART

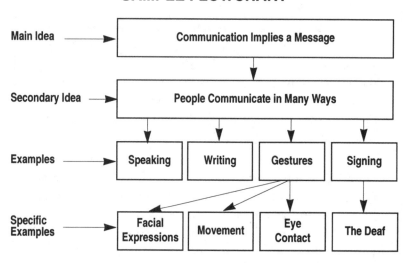

> > > INSIGHTS < < <

This activity requires close reading of the information in the passage. The organization imposed by the chart is not parallel to the organization of the original passage. However, the chart provides a logical organization for the ideas in a hierarchy which helps retention. The information the students have to transfer will probably be close to the key in the chart.

A possible activity which would allow students to go beyond the identification of main ideas and of supporting details and examples would consist of a reorganization of the passage according to the chart. This activity integrates several skills: the creation of a new passage by capitalizing on logical sequencing and outlining.

RECOGNIZING GENERALIZATIONS

When teaching students to recognize generalizations, we try to direct the student to the explicit propositions that sum up principles, facts, examples, and other supporting material. This skill is somewhat different from finding the main idea in that here we look for an explicitly stated principle. In locating main ideas we are not necessarily looking for an explicit principle.

Every expository text contains generalizations. They usually state a principle or a concept in very general terms and are followed by supporting details such as examples, illustrations, explanations, and definitions.

In class, have your students identify the generalizations in a text. There is no need to introduce special texts for this purpose, you can use any text you are working on. Pay attention to titles and subtitles, especially in journals and newspapers. Many times they contain generalizations.

RECOGNIZING EXAMPLES

The recognition of examples is an important skill. It enhances the comprehension of a text in a number of ways.

▶ Examples aid the understanding of concepts.
▶ Examples are used to illustrate more general ideas.
▶ Examples help make abstract ideas more concrete.
▶ Examples expand definitions.
▶ Examples make reading passages more vivid and closer to our own experience.

The student should recognize, however, that examples are used as support and not as the main point of the passage.

DISCOURSE MARKERS THAT SIGNAL EXAMPLES

> **for example, to illustrate, specifically, once, for instance, such as, e.g., common examples are, typical examples are, the main types are, its main uses are, its main parts are, its main components are**

What is typical of an example?

▶ It often follows a generalization.
▶ It may be positive or negative and in any tense.
▶ It tells about specific people, events of things.
▶ It sometimes tells a short story.
▶ It often includes expressions such as **that is, for instance.**

The activities suggested in this section are based on the following text. You may want to use a different text to suit your students' needs. The activities are easily applicable to most expository passages.

Building Materials

In most places there are numerous building materials to choose from. We can choose from more than a dozen materials for the outside walls. Many other materials can be used for roofs and floors and inside walls, for pipes and gutters and built-in furniture.

In other places, there are fewer materials to build with. Snow, driftwood, and skins, for instance, were the only materials an Eskimo could find in the past for building a shelter.

Stone is a natural building material. It only needs to be cut into the shape wanted. There are many kinds of stones. Those used most in building are limestone, marble, granite, sand-stone, and slate. Sometimes the stone is not even cut into shape. Rounded stones called field stones are used to make attractive walls.

Wood is another natural building material. There are many kinds of wood to choose from. Pine and oak are common. Snow, grass, palm leaves, and mud are natural building materials, too.

But many of our building materials are man-made. Brick, steel, glass, concrete, plywood, fiber board, and plaster are a few of them.

Some of the materials that are used in our buildings cannot be seen after the buildings are finished. When looking, for instance, at the great Empire State Building in New York City, no one would guess that a framework made of 57,000 tons of steel is hidden in its walls.

There are many things to think about in choosing the materials for a building. Here are some: How will they look? How long will they last? How much will they cost? How easy are they to maintain? Are they fireproof?

KEY WORDS

Key words facilitate the identification of the main points of a passage. Their recognition is important for the identification of main ideas, and by extension, to the identification of supporting details and examples.

 The purpose of this activity is to encourage students to infer the topic of the passage from key words before they are given the text. This pre-reading activity can be done as a whole class activity or in groups.

For this activity, divide the class into three groups. Each group gets a different list, with the following instructions: Read the list of words. They are all taken from a passage we are about to read. Try to guess what the topic of the passage is.

List A: Snow, skins, natural, stone, marble, wood, grass, leaves, steel, granite.

List B: Snow, skins, building, stone, sound, shape, marble, wood, leaves, grass.

List C: Snow, skins, building, stone, wall, roof, materials, wood, grass, brick.

Note: For list A the students will probably come up with "Natural Materials." For list B, they will come up with a variety of answers such as "Natural Surrounding," "Buildings & Climate," "Quality of Life." Only for list C will they say something about "Building Materials," "Development of Buildings," etc.

Class discussion: Why did group A miss the topic? (Reason: The words in the list are examples only; they do not express a main idea. They are connected to the topic, but they could be examples for many other things.)

Why did group B come closer to the topic? (Reason: The words in the list include some reference to the topic, but still, too many of them are examples).

Why did group C come very close to the topic? (Reason: Key words are included. Key words are topic words and refer directly to the subject under discussion).

MAIN IDEAS VS. EXAMPLES

Now, hand out the passage. Have each group underline the sentences containing the main idea of each paragraph. Note: Not all paragraphs have explicit main ideas. Sometimes, one must infer the main idea from the examples.

Point out to your students that the main idea of a paragraph may come at the beginning, middle, or end. However, in expository writing the main idea is generally stated at the beginning of the paragraph, and the explanations, examples, and illustrations follow and provide support for the generalization contained in the opening sentence.

Then, ask the students to locate the various examples. Discuss markers that helped them recognize the examples *(for instance, those used most are,... are a few of them, here are some)*.

Group work: Copy each topic sentence onto a separate card. Distribute one card to each group. Each group provides examples and explanations for their particular sentence on a clean sheet of paper. When they are done, have the groups exchange their lists with another group. Collect the original cards.

Each group now has some examples, provided by another group. Let them try to reconstruct the topic sentence.

Locating Examples in an Expository Text and Providing Examples from "Real Life"

ANIMAL HELP

Sometimes animals help people in unusual ways. For example, people in jail who are allowed to keep pets sometimes become less nervous. One doctor showed that heart patients who owned pets lived longer than heart patients who didn't have pets. This may be because pets helped these people relax.

Pets can be good companions. People who spend a lot of time alone often have pets as their closest friends. Many children also feel their pets are their best friends. As Joan Kemp, a teenager from Australia, says about her dog, "She's always there. She's always glad to see me, and she always forgives me."

Animals can be trained to help people. Dogs are used to find bombs and drugs. Police dogs attack when commanded. Dogs learn how to crawl through narrow places, jump over fences, and climb ladders. They learn how to obey instantly. Birds can be taught to carry mail. Monkeys can be trained to help people who are handicapped. For example, they are taught to turn on the lights, feed people, and even turn on a computer.

Sometimes animals help people in unusual ways. A dog in England discovered that his owner had a cancer on his leg. The dog barked at the leg, but his owner didn't pay attention. He didn't think it was serious. One day the dog bit the cancer. This time, the man had to go to the doctor. The doctor said, "It's lucky that you came. We must take care of this right away!" The dog saved his master's life. How did it know that it was a cancer? Researchers are now trying to find out more about such interesting cases.

POST READING Find five examples of "animal help" in the text. Do you know how animals help

▶ people who are blind?
▶ people who are lost?
▶ people who are lonely?
▶ people who are handicapped?
▶ people who are sick?
▶ people who are buried under the snow?
▶ people who are buried under ruins?

Give examples. [31]

▶▶▶ INSIGHTS ◀◀◀

Finding examples in a text (narrative or expository) is a valuable activity. As a while-reading activity it helps students focus on the details that support or illustrate the main ideas, arguments, or points. As a post-reading activity, it sends students back to the text and allows review and reinterpretation.

You may use almost any text for practice, and students may then use the examples found for various purposes, such as justifying their own interpretation, explaining their answers to information questions, or supporting their inferences.

GENERALIZATIONS VS. EXAMPLES OR SUPPORTING DETAILS

Your students should be aware that generalizations sum up facts and ideas presented by the author and are usually followed by examples and explanations. They should notice that the generalizations are often stated in the present simple.

Introductory activities

 SAMPLE ACTIVITY You may want to illustrate the difference between a generalization and supporting details by providing the class with the following generalizations. The class will provide four or five sentences giving supporting details.

1. Jim is a very attractive young man.
2. Tom is very rebellious.
3. Karen is not well brought up.

Ask each student to write an additional generalization followed by five supporting details.

 Finding the Generalization

A generalization states broad ideas. It doesn't include details. Examples are specific details. They are illustrations or explanations that come either before or after the generalization, the broad statement.

In each pair, find the generalization and the example.

 1.
   a. Water makes things seem to be where they are not.
   b. If you aim your fishing line at a fish where it seems to be, you will miss it.

 2.
   a. If you photograph the huge moon when it is low near the horizon, in the photograph, the moon will look very small.
   b. When the moon is near the horizon, it appears much larger than it appears when it is high in the sky.

3.
   a. We may see motion when there isn't any.
   b. When the moon is surrounded by moving clouds, it appears to race across the sky, while the clouds seem to stand still.

 4.
   a. Whenever there is movement, we have to decide what's moving and what isn't moving.
   b. In a moving car, it is sometimes hard to tell which car is moving — the car we are in, or the one next to us.

5.	a. Vertical lines on the wall make a ceiling look higher than it really is.
	b. Architects and home decorators often make use of optical illusions.

6.	a. Dress designers often make use of optical illusions.
	b. If you want to appear thinner than you really are, wear something with vertical lines. [32]

SAMPLE ACTIVITY: Text-Based Activity: Eliminating Irrelevant Examples

Fighting for a Better Environment

For centuries people felt that nature was theirs. They acted as if the plants and animals on our planet were unlimited. However, as civilization became more complex, the threat to animal and plant life became more serious. People have destroyed many animals and plants and have polluted the air and the seas.

In recent times, however, people have become more concerned about the future of our planet. More and more people are protesting against the thoughtless destruction of our environment. They have formed organizations that fight to save all forms of life. People from different parts of the world are joining together to save the world.

They work to protect the environment and to stop the needless killing of animals. They warn the world that environmental pollution is a serious danger. They fight to protect and to clean up the air, the water, and the land. They want to keep the world a safe place for all living things. They warn against the dangers caused by modern technology.

The main purpose of environmental organizations is to make people aware of dangers that might change the balance of nature. Some organizations provide news for television stations. Others try to push laws against environmental pollution. People of different countries have joined together because environmental problems are not usually problems of one nation but of many.

The largest environmental organization is called Greenpeace. This organization encourages cooperation on environmental problems among nations. It has 2.5 million members from all over the world. Thousands of volunteers work for Greenpeace.

They fight for clean seas. They try to stop the development of the nuclear-power industry. They try to protect marine animals. Greenpeace volunteers fight against oil drilling near shores. They fight to keep Antarctica unchanged. They fight against the burning of dangerous wastes. They fight against pollution and acid rain. They try to prevent factories from throwing away dangerous wastes into rivers and seas. They fight the killing of kangaroos in Australia. They do everything that they can to make the world a better place to live in.

 POST READING The following are generalizations made in the text. Each is followed by supporting details. Some details and examples belong, and others do not. Which details do not support the generalization?

1. For centuries people have felt that nature was theirs.
   a. They fight to protect the air, the water, and the land.
   b. They have destroyed many animals and plants.
   c. They have polluted the air and the seas.
   d. They have 2.5 million members from all over the world.

2. Environmental organizations fight to save all forms of life.
   a. The threat to animal and plant life has become more serious.
   b. They fight the killing of kangaroos in Australia.

c. They fight to protect and to clean up the air.

d. They try to protect marine animals.

e. They work to stop the needless killing of animals.

3. The main purpose of environmental organizations is to make people aware of the danger that nature is in.

    a. They provide news for television stations.

    b. Environmental problems are not usually problems of one nation but of many.

    c. They try to push laws against environmental pollution.

    d. People of different countries have joined together.

4. Environmental organizations fight to save the world.

    a. They fight for clean seas.

    b. They try to stop the development of the nuclear-power industry.

    c. They have become concerned about the future of the planet.

    d. They fight against oil drilling near shores.

    e. They fight to keep Antarctica unchanged.

    f. They fight against the burning of dangerous wastes.

    g. They fight against air pollution and acid rain.

    h. They try to prevent factories from throwing dangerous wastes into rivers and seas. [33]

▶▶▶ INSIGHTS ◀◀◀

By eliminating details which do not support the generalization, students will see the logical connection between the generalization and the supporting materials.

Providing Examples to Illustrate Generalizations

This activity illustrates the relationship between generalizations and examples. Note the example markers provided.

Illustrate each generalization by providing a suitable example from real life.

1. Climate seems to have an influence on behavior. For example, …

2. We often change plans and activities because of weather conditions. For example, …

3. Our moods also change with the weather. A good example for this would be …

4. Bright sunny days seem to make people happy. For instance, …

5. Dark rainy periods cause depression. A typical example is …[34]

You may give other generalizations based on students' experiences and their environment, this time without the markers.

▶ Modern technology can be used in teaching.

▶ It is sometimes hard to understand the news.

▶ Many people panic in dangerous situations.

▶ Teenagers and adults may have communication problems.

▶ Modern education doesn't always train people for jobs.

READING FOR FACTUAL INFORMATION

There are certain types of reading material that must be read for factual information, such as tourist guides, cook books, instructions of various types, and time-tables. Reading for factual information is part of social studies, science and other school subjects.

The most common activity types for finding facts in texts are the following:

1. Wh-questions such as *When, Where, What happened? How? Who said what and why?*

2. True or False, or yes or no questions, and multiple choice questions, which should be carefully constructed so that the distractors are not too far-fetched or too close to the actual facts in the text.

 **Wh-Questions Activity**

APPOINTMENT IN SAMARRA
by W. Somerset Maugham

There was a merchant in Baghdad who sent his servant to market to buy food, and in a little while the servant came back, white and trembling, and said, "Master, just now when I was in the marketplace, I was jostled by a woman in the crowd, and when I turned, I saw it was Death that jostled me. She looked at me and made a threatening gesture. Please lend me your horse, and I

---

will ride away from this city and avoid my fate. I will go to Samarra, and there Death will not find me."

The merchant lent him his horse, and the servant mounted it, and he dug his spurs in its flanks, and as fast as the horse could gallop he went.

Then the merchant went down to the marketplace, and he saw Death standing in the crowd, and he came to Death and said, "Why did you make a threatening gesture to my servant when you saw him this morning?" "That was not a threatening gesture," Death said. "It was only a start of surprise. I was astonished to see him in Baghdad, for I had an appointment with him tonight in Samarra."

POST READING

Answer the questions that follow:

1. Why did the servant come back white and trembling?
2. Why did the servant ask for his master's horse?
3. Why did the servant dig his spurs into the horse's flanks?
4. Why did Death make a gesture to the servant?
5. Why was Death astonished? [35]

To scan is to look for specific information quickly. When you scan, you don't read every word.

 Scan the table that follows. Answer these questions as fast as you can.

1. How many animals have wings?
2. Which reptile is mentioned?
3. How many insects are mentioned?
4. How many farm animals are there?
5. Which animals have no legs?
6. Which name is used only for a young animal?
7. How many animals are long?
8. What is special about the duck?
9. How many desert animals are mentioned?
10. How many animals that have 6 legs are mentioned?
11. Complete this report. Write numbers.

In our table we have_____mammals, _____insects, _____ reptiles, _____birds and _____fish. We have _____two-legged animals, _____four-legged animals, _____six-legged animals, _____animals without legs and _____animals with wings.

ANIMAL	SPECIES	NUMBER OF LIMBS	HOME	CHARACTERISTICS
bear	mammal	4 legs	cave	big, hairy, sleeps through the winter, good parent
bee	insect	6 legs & wings	hive	makes honey
camel	mammal	4 legs	desert	humped back, long neck, stores fat, can go two weeks without water
cat	mammal	4 legs	homes & farms	color-blind, purrs, eats mice, domesticated
chicken	bird	2 legs & wings	farm	can't fly high
cow	mammal	4 legs	farm	raised for its milk
dog	mammal	4 legs	homes & farms	intelligent, colorblind, domesticated, good sense of smell
dolphin	mammal	fins	water	has teeth, breathes air, lives in groups, intelligent
donkey	mammal	4 legs	farm	stubborn, domesticated, means of transportation
duck	bird	2 legs & wings	in & near water	swimming bird, has a flat beak
elephant	mammal	4 legs & trunk	jungle	largest land animal, thick skin, no hair, can be domesticated
fly	insect	6 legs & 2 wings	in & around house	eats garbage, spreads disease
horse	mammal	4 legs	farm	domesticated, used for transportation

kangaroo	mammal	2 long hind legs & 2 short forelegs	land	long thick tail, native of Australia, babies kept in pouch
lamb	mammal	4 legs	farm	young sheep, has wool
lion	mammal	4 legs	jungle	cat family, large, strong
monkey	mammal	2 arms & 2 legs	land	very developed, intelligent, has a tail
mosquito	insect	6 legs & 2 wings	near water	the female bites, sucks blood, carries disease, 1000 kinds
mouse	mammal	4 legs	land	very small, long, thin tail
pig	mammal	4 legs	farm	fat body, short legs, short tail
rat	mammal	4 legs	land	lives almost anywhere, carries disease, long tail
shark	fish	fins	water	over 150 different kinds, cold-blooded, hard skin, fish-eater
sheep	mammal	4 legs	farm	heavy wool, eats grass
snake	reptile	no legs	land or water	long, no lids on eyes, sheds its skin
tiger	mammal	4 legs	land	cat family, eats meat, large
zebra	mammal	4 legs	land	has stripes, wild, native of Africa

36

▶▶▶ INSIGHTS ◀◀◀

You may want to show the class how to scan efficiently. Do one as an example, and explain that to answer question 1 we need to go to the right column (limbs) and quickly scan down the column, looking for the word "wings." It is not efficient to read all the information in the table. The key is to look for the information that we need.

Conduct an experiment. Tell students to scan a list from bottom to top. Ask them if they find it harder than scanning from top to bottom. They probably do. We are used to going from top to bottom just as we are used to scanning texts from left to right. Students who are used to different alphabetical systems may scan differently..

 Scanning a Time Line

A TIME LINE

1800	**1802**	John Dalton developed his atomic theory.
1850	**1895**	Roentgen discovered x-rays.
1900	**1902**	The Curies discovered radium.
	1903	The theory of the empty atom was developed.
	1904	A Japanese scientist, Hantaro Nagaoka, developed a model of the atom.
1910	**1913**	Niels Bohr developed his model of the atom.
1920		
1930	**1930**	The first atom smasher was built. Modern nuclear science began.

A time line shows things in the order that they happened. This time line shows important events in the history of atomic science. Use the time line to decide if the sentences are right or wrong.

yes no

☐ ☐ Bohr and Dalton knew each other.
☐ ☐ Bohr's model of the atom is older than Dalton's model.
☐ ☐ Someone smashed atoms in the 19th century.
☐ ☐ Dalton's theory is older than the Japanese theory.
☐ ☐ The Curies discovered radium at the beginning of the 20th century.

☐	☐	Radium was discovered before the discovery of x-rays.
☐	☐	Modern nuclear theory started in the 1930's.
☐	☐	John Dalton lived in the 18th century.
☐	☐	The Curies and Bohr lived in the same century.
☐	☐	The theory of the empty atom is older than the Japanese model.
☐	☐	When John Dalton was sick, he had an x-ray to find out the problem. [37]

Note: Scanning is facilitated by the chronological sequence of the information. Capitalization facilitates scanning for names.

 **The Scanning Game**

The following activity is based on the chronological list on page 80.

Scan the information in "Important Steps in the Development of Mass Communication" on page 80.

Answer the following questions as **quickly** as you can.
Do one question at a time. Time yourself. The winner is the group or the student that gets **all** the items right in the shortest time.

> 1. Which items are about newspapers?
> 2. Which items are about paper making?
> 3. How many items are about the movies?
> 4. Which items are about the radio?
> 5. When was the first television program?
> 6. When was the first book printed?
> 7. How many times does the word "telephone" appear?
> 8. How many years passed between the first television program and the beginning of color television?
> 9. What was the name of the first English newspaper?
> 10. When did a person speak over the radio for the first time? [38]

Note: The time element encourages fast scanning and discourages slow, linear reading.

The comprehension of factual information is especially important in reading informative texts such as advertisements. These announcements are meant to convince the reader to do something and to inform the reader about certain properties and qualities of the advertised item.

 Find A House For Them

Read the ads and find a suitable house for each person. The home must satisfy the person's needs and taste. You may choose the same home for more than one person.

VILLAS AND HIDEAWAYS

Cave. Leave it all behind. Try a new beginning. Move into an almost real cave. Dim lights. Moving walls. Hard to find. Running water. Food supply for 8 months.

A mud house. Go to the Gobi desert. No running water. No electricity. No traffic problems. No skyscrapers. Helicopter service provided. Call: 1-800-555-1254.

No corners! Round kitchen. Round bedrooms. Round terrace. Soft colors. Music out of the walls. Young neighborhood. Vegetable garden. Good schools. Reasonable. Write: P.O.B. 35667.

Desert island. Beautiful view. Sharks keep away the unwanted. Palm tree park. Discreet servant. Telephone, FAX and telex service. Call: Friday.

Haunted house. Real ghosts! Windows creak in the wind. Bugs, spiders and frogs. Good for a movie set. Can be fixed up.

Live in a gift box. Every day is your birthday. Beautiful villa shaped like a present. Ribbons and bows all around. Pink! Heart-shaped swimming pool with sweet water. Large dining area. Over the age of 25 only.

PENTHOUSES AND CITY LIVING

Underground apartment. No noise. Police protection 24 hours a day. No pollution. 50 yards below Spring Park. Telephone: 415-692-1285.

Star-shaped house. Modern electronic Equipment. House repair robot. The country in the middle of the city. Write and send references: #3345.

Penthouse. 158th floor. Center of town. Cleaning service. Clouds down below. Luxurious. No dogs allowed.

NATURE LOVERS

Plastic house. Almost like living outdoors. On the beach for all to see. Transparent walls and furniture. No privacy.

Floating river house. No pollution. Hydroelectric. Good people. Nature lovers. Children invited. Swimmers only. Really cheap.

Cottage. Small and cozy. No stairs. Talking furniture. Automated service. Medical service by phone.

HOUSES WANTED

1. Businessman. Wants to go on a vacation where no one can reach him. Especially the bank. Has many enemies.

2. Popstar. Very wealthy. Hates to commute. Goes everywhere with his dog. Needs the city.

3. Career woman. Doesn't have much free time. Wants a central location. Quiet surroundings. Hobby: flying.

4. Swimming teacher. Mother of 3, enjoys other people, fights pollution. Not too rich.

5. Millionaire. Hates people, especially children. Likes privacy. Must be in touch with his office in the city at all times.

6. Family with 6 children. Two dogs and a cat. Noisy but sweet natured. Very wealthy. Like comfort. Good schools required.

7. Filmmakers. Looking for mysterious places. Collect stray dogs and cats. Interested in making a movie about witches.

8. Traveling guitar player. Must have water and sun. Friendly, likes outdoor living.

9. Allergic to flowers, trees and insects. Looking for good solution.

10. After accident. Broken leg. Need comfort, service, and medical care.

11. Retired actress. Very sentimental. Looking for something to express her personality. Entertains a lot.

12. Tired of it all! Peace and quiet! No modern equipment. No news! No telephone! Transportation required.

13. Writer. Needs privacy for 6 months.

14. Traveling salesman. Looking for temporary home. Willing to share.

₃₉

▶▶▶ INSIGHTS ◀◀◀

To complete this activity successfully, students must pay close attention to the information provided in the two sets of ads and then match them. This exercise emulates real-life situations where people have to make decisions on the basis of information they have read.

Follow up this activity with short descriptions of real people, e.g., famous people or class members. Decide what their needs are.

Bring in the classified ads of a local newspaper and have students match ads to people. You can do this for a variety of ad types such as ads for jobs, cars, or houses.

 **Reading a Product Label**

Read the following information and answer the questions:

The Keep-a-life Tablet

Each tablet contains

Pro-life	500 mg
Cucumber and carrot extract	200 mg
Powdered frog extract	10 mg
Deer horn extract	2 mg

Therapeutic activity
Prevents death of all kinds.

Dosage
To be used as directed by physician.
Do not exceed the recommended dosage.
Normal dosage: 1 tablet three times daily.
This medication should be taken on an
empty stomach (one hour before meals).
Do not stop using this medicine unless
directed by physician.

Warnings
Do not give to children under 12.
If you are over 120 years old, do not
take this medicine.
The doctor should be informed if you
suffer from headaches, dizziness, or
strange, violent behavior.
This medication should be taken by
human beings only! Do not give to
animals or any other life forms.

Side Effects
All drugs may have undesirable side
effects. If you feel a change in your
general health, call your doctor, who
will advise you.
In the event of death, our company will
refund the cost of the medicine and pay
for all funeral expenses.

Storage
This medicine should be kept in a cool
and dry place. It should be kept out of
reach of small children.

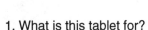

POST READING

1. What is this tablet for?

2. When and how often should you take it?

3. Three groups should not take Keep-A-Life tablets. What are they?

   a.

   b.

   c. [40]

Note: This activity is based on a mock leaflet. However, it is very much like original leaflets of the same kind. Grasping detailed information here is of vital importance.

THE LAWS OF HEREDITY

Before a baby is born, we can sometimes guess what color eyes it will have. If one parent has brown eyes and the other has blue eyes, the child will usually have brown eyes. If the parents don't have any brown pigment in their eyes, the child will have blue eyes. If one of the parents has curly hair, the child will have a 50-50 chance of having curly hair. However, the laws of heredity aren't simple. We don't really know what a child will look like until it is born.

Genetics is a branch of biology that studies heredity. Genes that come from the mother and from the father give the child special characteristics. We have 23 pairs of chromosomes in every cell. The chromosomes come from both the father and the mother. There are thousands of genes in the chromosomes. Do you see why the laws of heredity aren't simple?

 POST READING **There are many facts in this passage.** Check the facts that are **new to you.**

❑ If one parent has brown eyes and the other has blue eyes, the child will usually have brown eyes.

❑ If the parents don't have any brown pigment in their eyes, the child will have blue eyes.

❑ If one of the parents has curly hair, the child will have a 50-50 chance of having curly hair.

❑ We don't really know what a baby will look like until it is born.

❑ Genes come from the mother and from the father. They give the child special characteristics.

❑ Genetics is a branch of biology that studies heredity.

❑ We have 23 pairs of chromosomes in every cell.

❑ The chromosomes come from both the father and the mother.

❑ There are thousands of genes in the chromosomes. [41]

FACT FINDING AND CLASSIFICATION

The following activity is based on the text, "**What is Communication,**" pp. 105-106.

  Which of the following are necessary for communicating with other people?

	NECESSARY	USEFUL	NOT NECESSARY
1. eye contact			
2. a sender			
3. a receiver			
4. a message			
5. gestures			
6. telepathy			
7. a telephone			
8. language			
9. facial expressions			
10. voice			
11. words			
12. signs			
13. hearing			
14. sight			
15. sentences			

[42]

 ▶▶▶ INSIGHTS ◀◀◀

If used as post reading, this activity demands that students go back to the text, check the information again and classify it.

SAMPLE ACTIVITY Fortune Telling

Read these predictions.

1. Keep away from business decisions. This is not your week.
2. You will soon meet someone interesting.
3. You may have family problems this week.
4. Something unexpected will happen to you this week.
5. This is your week for traveling! Take an interesting trip.
6. Things will get better for you next week.
7. Don't lend your things to anyone this month. You won't get them back.
8. Someone close to you will need your help this week.
9. You are on your way to great success.
10. Don't throw away any papers this week. You will need them in the future.
11. Listen to people even if they don't seem helpful to you.
12. Take care of your health this week. Pay attention to the weather.
13. You will hear some good news this week.
14. You will get an interesting letter.

 POST READING Try to find...

1. one prediction that is not new to you.

2. one prediction that is sure to happen to you.

3. one prediction which gives advice.

4. one prediction that you might accept.

5. one prediction that warns you of possible risks.

6. one prediction that is optimistic.

7. one prediction that is pessimistic.

If these predictions actually take place, what will you do this coming week? Check the appropriate column.

POST READING	I will	I won't	I am not sure
1. make business decisions			
2. try to meet someone interesting			
3. speak to my family			
4. travel			
5. lend something to someone			
6. help someone			
7. throw away papers			
8. listen to people			
9. listen to the news			
10. check my mail box			

CLASSIFICATION, COMPARISON, AND CONTRAST

The analysis of a text very often demands that we classify information. Authors often provide a classification of their main ideas by divisions within the text (subtitles, paragraphs) or by some internal organization (to begin with, first, then, after that, to summarize, etc., cf. Logical Sequencing). At other times, no such guidance is provided, and it is left to the reader to find those classifications present in the text. Classification is therefore a very broad topic depending on what is being classified: the topics, the ideas, the concepts, or the examples.

Comparisons and contrasts are one way of classifying information. Here the classification is achieved through a presentation of similarities and differences.

Some of the activities in this section lend themselves for use with a computer database. If such a program is used in your school, you may ask your students to enter the information gathered into the database and later retrieve that information according to various classifications or criteria.

DISCOURSE MARKERS THAT SIGNAL COMPARISON AND CONTRAST

Comparison: likewise, similarly, in the same way, like, in comparison, also, too.

Contrast: but, however, in contrast, despite this, in spite of, yet, instead, although, even though, otherwise, still, on the contrary, on the one hand, on the other hand, conversely, nevertheless, actually, as a matter of fact, at the same time, unlike, whereas, while, not that, except that.

Note that the contrasts and oppositions may vary in format, focus, and degree of balance.

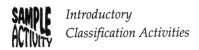 *Introductory*
Classification Activities

> Materials are different from each other. For example, some are solids, others are liquids, and others gases. By looking at the materials, smelling them or touching them, you can learn what their characteristics are. We can classify materials by their characteristics and in fact different materials can belong to different groups, depending on the classifying characteristic that is used.

a. Classify the list of materials according to consistency, color, taste, size, form, etc. Each time use different characteristics and see how the materials group.

List of materials: coal, wax, vinegar, carbon-dioxide, wood, stone, salt, syrup, milk, water, rubber, sponges, glass, bronze, steam, ...(add any others)

List of characteristics: hard or soft, rough or smooth, flexible or rigid, sweet or sour, edible or inedible, solid, liquid or gas, ...(add any others)

b. Make lists of foods, drinks, animals, flowers, furniture, nationalities, etc. Then classify them according to different criteria.

▶▶▶ INSIGHTS ◀◀◀

The purpose of this activity is to make students aware of the various ways in which data can be organized. The assumption is that by helping students recognize the organizational structure of a set of lists, one prepares them for grasping the organization or structure of a text. This awareness of organization and hierarchies is very useful in understanding what we read.

Awareness of Similarities and Differences

 **Explorers Look Alike**

An astronaut, a modern fighter pilot, a mountain climber, and a sea diver look alike when dressed for their exploration.

a. Why do you think that is so?

b. Check all those boxes that you believe are right.

c. Discuss your table with your classmates.

d. Write a paragraph comparing any two by using the information in the table.

NEEDS	ASTRONAUT	PILOT	MOUNTAIN CLIMBER	SEA DIVER
protective clothes				
breathing tubes				
a supply of air				
a controlled, constant temperature				

 Vegetables

Every vegetable we eat is a part of a plant. A vegetable may be the root, bulb, stem, leaves, flowers, seeds, or fruit. The list below names some of the vegetables that we eat. What part of the plant do we eat in each case? Check the appropriate column.

	root	bulb	leaves	flowers	seeds	fruit
artichoke						
bean						
beet						
cabbage						
spinach						
pepper						
tomato						
onion						
eggplant						
carrot						
cauliflower						

What else do you know about these vegetables? What is their color? What is their consistency? Use the information that you have to write a paragraph in which you compare and contrast any two vegetables.

The following words will help you: **hard, tender, bitter, sweet, orange, green.**

►►► INSIGHTS ◄◄◄

These activities are not text-based, but they could precede or follow a reading activity. The "skeleton" is provided in the form of a table, and students fill in the information based on their prior knowledge if the activity is done as pre-reading or based on the information in the text if done as post-reading. The writing activity has reading as an aim. By writing a paragraph of comparison, students become aware of how such passages are organized, which in turn will help them comprehend.

Identifying Explicit Comparisons and Contrasts

Read the following text on rabbits and hares; pay attention to the boldfaced words.

Rabbits and Hares

Rabbits make good pets. They are also kept for their fur and, in some parts of the world, for their meat. Rabbits dig burrows. They live in colonies and breed rapidly.

Hares look **like** rabbits, **but** they are **bigger**, with **longer** ears and legs. Hares are swift runners. **Unlike** rabbits, they live alone and do not dig burrows. **Instead**, they live in hollows in the ground.

 In the list below, decide who the information is about—rabbits or hares.

_____ They live in hollows in the ground.

_____ They live in colonies.

_____ They are kept as pets.

_____ They are swift runners.

_____ They dig burrows.

_____ Their ears are long.

_____ They live alone.

Note: It is possible to give your students the list first, and then let them read the passage to check their classification.

The Computer

Machines can usually do only one thing. A washing machine can wash clothes, a dishwasher can wash dishes, and a vacuum cleaner can suck up dirt.

The computer is different. It can do many things. We can use computers in business, in education, and for playing games. Many schools, offices, factories, and homes have computers. Why is the computer so useful? The difference between computers and other machines is the program. The program can change the computer from a game machine into a teaching machine, from an office machine into an engineering machine. The program "tells" the computer what to do. The program is a set of instructions. The computer can "understand" the instructions very quickly, but it cannot think. It cannot do anything without a program.

---

1. The computer is different from the vacuum cleaner.

 What are these sentences about?

Write: **The computer** or **The vacuum cleaner**.

1._____ can clean the rug.
2._____ can understand a program.
3._____ can do many things.
4._____ can teach English.
5._____ can solve math problems.
6._____ can vacuum the sofa.
7._____ can remember students' grades.
8._____ can show information.

2. Where do the following words belong?

Some of the words fit more than one column.

addresses	clean	clothes	coats	cups
dirt	diskettes	dishes	dresses	dust
floors	grades	glasses	instructions	neat
numbers	rugs	sofas	to vacuum	wash
water	to write			

Computer	Vacuum Cleaner	Dishwasher	Washing Machine
_____	_____	_____	_____
_____	_____	_____	_____
_____	_____	_____	_____
_____	_____	_____	_____
_____	_____	_____	_____

44

SAMPLE ACTIVITY

The Teleprompter

Television announcers and actors do not need to memorize a lot of information. Actually, they only read it. Some read from a device called a teleprompter. Others prefer to read from a typed page.

The teleprompter is attached to the camera so that the performer can read while looking directly into the camera. This device shows the words in very large type so it can be read easily. The audience usually can't tell if the person is reading the words from the teleprompter because it seems as if she is looking directly into the camera.

A typed page, on the other hand, is held in the hands or lies on the desk. The words are usually printed in large letters so it is very easy to read. People who use a typed page have to look down at it instead of always looking into the camera.

How are the teleprompter and a typed page the same, and how are they different? Check similar or different in the table according to the information in the reading passage. Then explain your choices giving support from the passage.

	Similar	Different
function		
location		
size of print		
effect on viewer		

**THE INTELLIGENT ANTI-CRIME
HOUSE OF THE FUTURE**

A People have always tried to protect their homes against crime. In the past, people protected their private homes by building high walls around them, by planting thick bushes and trees, or by digging canals. Some people used dogs and guards to protect their homes. At present, houses are protected by computer-operated systems, locks, fences, and police patrols. Most modern homes have large windows and good lighting; therefore, it is easy to see people coming near the house. Many buildings already use closed circuit television to watch the area outside the building.

B In the past, fortresses were built with very thick walls. Some walls were two meters thick! Nowadays, we can use very strong materials to build secure buildings. The walls don't need to be thick, but they must be made of hard, long-lasting materials.

C In the future, homes will probably be much more secure than they are today. Today's computers can already recognize voices and even "see." Tomorrow's computers will be much more powerful. They will be able to process large amounts of information and make decisions based on this information. The use of computer technology will make homes secure and therefore reduce crime. As a result, the quality of life will improve.

D Security systems will be used to prevent strangers from entering. The system will automatically check all the doors and windows. The security system will even be able to tell if the person approaching the house is a friend, a relative, a stranger, a child, or a pet. Computer sensors will be able to detect movement, body heat, electromagnetic fields, sounds, and sizes. They will check if there is information about the visitor in the memory of the computer. The computer will then decide what to do next. A computer voice may politely tell a visitor that he cannot enter the building, or the computer may recognize the voice patterns of a known criminal and automatically alert the police.

E Doors in the future will not be like today's doors. They will be made of very strong, thin materials. These materials will be unbreakable and fire-proof. Each door will have a system that will control the air coming in from the outside. Doors will be opened not only by keys or magnetic cards, but also by voice commands or by infrared or microwave sensors.

F Windows will be made of materials that are light, unbreakable, and easy to install. Built-in sensors will inform the house computer if a window is opened from the outside, and an alarm will go off.

G In the 21st century, houses will not only be safe, they will be intelligent. Each room will be monitored for temperature and humidity. A computer will note the location of each person in the house. It may keep track of the family's schedule or even the pet's needs. For example, the computer will know that the youngest child is expected back from school at 1 o'clock, and that the door must be opened for the cat at 6 o'clock a.m. and again at 6 o'clock p.m. It will remind owners of their shopping needs. For example, it may announce: "No milk in the refrigerator. The batteries in the music system need to be replaced by tomorrow." The time may come when it will even announce, "You're tired. Time to go to bed."

H The house of the future will be equipped with high technology, and therefore, it will be much more secure. However, we must ask ourselves: Will we be prisoners of our own security systems? How will technology affect our social lives? In the future, we will depend more and more on technology to solve our problems. Will the result be loneliness? Will the price for security be isolation?

Paragraph **A**
1. What is being compared in this paragraph?

Paragraph **B**
2. What two elements are contrasted in this paragraph?

3. What is the difference between the two? Write your explanation.

Paragraphs **E & F**
4. Complete the following table. Use the information in the passage and your own knowledge.

	present doors	future doors	present windows	future windows
materials				
ways to lock and unlock				

5. **Compare and contrast house protection in the past, the present, and the future.** Use the information in the following table to write at least one paragraph.

Past	Present	Future
high walls, water canals, thick fences, dogs	locks, fences police patrols closed circuit TV, dogs	intelligent house computers

6. **Compare and contrast something in the past, present and future.** You may use one of the following items or choose your own.

- ▶ Life in cities
- ▶ Social life
- ▶ Crime
- ▶ Inventions
- ▶ Teenage Fashion
- ▶ Food [45]

In these activities students are made aware of the explicit markers of comparison and contrast that can help them locate similarities and differences. The texts illustrate a variety of difficulty levels.

DEFINITIONS

A definition is the formal statement of the meaning of a word or a concept. Definitions must be concise and relevant because they deal with the important characteristics of the concept. By recognizing definitions, students will focus attention on the significant points to be considered in the text.

DISCOURSE MARKERS THAT SIGNAL DEFINITIONS

> X is defined as, we can/may define X as, in this context X is, for our purposes X is, we may say that X is, for the purpose of this paper, we can consider X means ...

Note that definitions are often marked in texts by punctuation marks such as a comma (Infrared light waves, the waves that are on the right side of the spectrum...,) a colon or a semicolon. In some cases, the expressions "that is" or "i.e." are used as definition markers (Infrared light waves, that is / i.e., the waves that are on the right side of the spectrum...,).

Consciousness-Raising Activities: The Parts of a Definition

The purpose of this activity is to teach the three parts of a typical definition: the concept (A car is...), the class (...a vehicle), the characteristics and examples (...that has a motor, a steering wheel and four wheels and is used to transport things and people from one place to another).

Prepare cards and label them as *concept, class* or *characteristics*. Each student gets a card. Then he/she looks for those students who have the missing portions of his/her definition. You now have three students in a group. Each group chooses one representative to read out loud. This student tries to elicit the concept from the class by reading only the contents of the card labeled *class*. If the class fails to guess, the characteristics are read.

Sample cards:

CONCEPT	**CLASS**
1. A car is ...	1. an electrical appliance
2. A dog is ...	2. a fruit
3. A lamp is ...	3. an instrument
4. A telephone is ...	4. an animal
5. An orange is ...	5. a vehicle

CHARACTERISTICS AND/OR EXAMPLES

1. that has a motor, a steering wheel and four wheels and is used to transport things or people from one place to another.
2. that has a tail and four legs, is a house pet and is considered man's best friend.
3. that has a transmitter and a receiver, and is used to transmit the voice of one person in one place to another person in another place.
4. that has an orange-colored peel and edible parts inside.
5. that has an electric bulb and a stand, gives light, and is often placed on a desk or on the floor.

 **Examining Dictionary Definitions**

1. Identify the three parts of definitions (concept, class, and characteristics) in dictionary definitions.

2. Write definitions for words that you know and compare them to dictionary definitions.

3. Identify definitions in a passage read in class. How are they different from dictionary definitions?

4. Discuss definitions in general. Which words are easy to define? (compare "sun" to "table" to "happiness"). Issues such as abstract ideas, ambiguous notions, etc., will surely come up.

5. In groups, make up your own definitions. Then compare them to the dictionary definitions.

For this activity choose vocabulary items from the unit you are now teaching. Besides learning about definitions, the new vocabulary will be reinforced.

 Vocabulary Introduction through Definitions

Use the following words to complete the definitions. Look up the words that you don't understand in the dictionary.

> alarm, canal, fortress, humidity, long-lasting, microwaves, monitor, sensor

1. An _____ is a sound which warns of danger.

2. _____ is the amount of water in the air.

3. To _____ is to check or watch what is happening.

4. A _____ is a strong and well protected building.

5. _____ are waves that produce heat. They are used for cooking, photography, and other things.

6. A _____ is an instrument that detects and records changes in heat and movement.

7. A _____ is a man-made water way.

8. A _____ object is an object that can be used for a long time. [46]

 SAMPLE ACTIVITY *Using a Database to Write Definitions*

The following activity is based on the table on pp. 122-123.

Use the data in the table to write definitions of animals.

Example: A bee is an insect that lives in a hive and makes honey.

Preparing Crossword Puzzles

Prepare a "skeleton" for a cross-word puzzle. Fill it in with familiar words. Divide class into groups and give filled-in crossword puzzles to class (a different one for each group). Have students prepare suitable definitions for all the items. Exchange definitions and have another group try to do the puzzle according to the definitions. Obviously, you will need an empty "skeleton" for each filled-in puzzle you use.

What Is the Greenhouse Effect?

A greenhouse is a glass or plastic building in which the temperature and humidity are controlled so plants have the best possible conditions. The warmth of the sunlight is kept inside by the glass or the plastic.

The Earth is kept warm by the atmosphere. The atmosphere acts very much like the glass of a greenhouse. Some natural gases in the atmosphere are warming gases. These gases form a "blanket" which allows sunlight to enter but does not allow all of the heat in the atmosphere to escape back into outer space. They prevent the Earth from reflecting solar heat back into space. This result is called the greenhouse effect.

Planets that do not have "greenhouse protection" may be much colder than Earth. Without the greenhouse effect, the Earth would be 33 degrees cooler, and it would be covered by ice.

Human activities have increased the amount of natural gases in the atmosphere. Modern developments have also created synthetic gases. The atmosphere is now holding in more heat than it used to. This added heat is known as global warming. Global warming has changed the heat balance of our planet.

POST READING Complete the following definitions.

1. The atmosphere is the envelope surrounding the _____. It consists of many gases.

2. Outer space is the space beyond the _____ of the Earth.

3. Solar heat is heat that comes from the _____.

4. A greenhouse is a glass or plastic building in which the _____ and humidity can be regulated.

5. The greenhouse effect is the phenomenon that prevents the Earth from reflecting _____ back into _____.

6. Global warming is the increase of heat in the _____.

7. Natural gases are gases that are found in the_____.

8. Synthetic gases are gases made by _____. [47]

▶▶▶ INSIGHTS ◀◀◀

The purpose of this activity is twofold. It reinforces the vocabulary encountered in the reading passage, and it provides practice in using definitions.

Chapter Seven

▶ ▶

Processes of Unification

The aim of the activities in this section is to help the student realize that certain parts of the text belong together, are unified in one way or another, and are consistent with one another. This realization allows the reader to recognize a variety of logical relations such as cause and effect, addition and contrast, and anaphoric relations. The recognition of unity or coherence also directs the reader's attention to chronological and logical sequencing. All these strategies, together with those in the previous chapters, facilitate the reader's ability to summarize whole passages or parts of them.

COHERENCE AND COHESION

These two terms are related to properties that make the text a unified whole. The two terms refer to both text characteristics and readers' interaction with the text.

Coherence is the means by which ideas, concepts, and propositions in a text are made to belong conceptually to the whole. It is the result of an interaction between the knowledge presented in the text and the reader's stored knowledge. As such, it is a quality that makes a text conform to a consistent world picture, to experiences, culture. and convention. If the text is incoherent, readers do not perceive it as a text.

Cohesion refers to the linguistic means by which elements of a text are arranged and connected. Cohesion relies heavily on grammatical devices in written discourse. Cohesion involves surface evidence, that is, readers can identify cohesive devices in the text provided that their linguistic knowledge is sufficient. Cohesion is therefore text-based, and its perception depends on the reader's knowledge of language.

LOGICAL RELATIONS IN TEXTS

▶ Students should realize that certain parts of the text belong together, that they are unified and consistent.

▶ Recognition of logical relations demands high cognitive skills such as textual associations and chaining of ideas which may prove difficult in a foreign language.

▶ The recognition of explicit markers will facilitate the comprehension of logical relationships.

Comprehension of logical relations is influenced, among other things, by the following:

Reader factors:
▶ reasoning abilities
▶ world knowledge
▶ background knowledge (topic related)
▶ cultural or social background
▶ syntactic knowledge
▶ level of interest

Text factors:

- ❱ discourse characteristics: genre, level of formality, etc.
- ❱ prominence of relation in the discourse
- ❱ amount of redundancy in the text
- ❱ presence or absence of explicit markers
- ❱ globality or locality of the relationship

 ## Awareness of Coherence: Identifying Incoherent Elements

There is one sentence in each story that doesn't belong. Cross it out.

a. Mary is learning German. She went to the movies yesterday. She always does her homework. She loves the language, and that's because she has a wonderful teacher.

b. Last year George went to Greece on holiday. He flew to Athens and then took a plane to Corfu. He knows Russian. He had a very good time and loved every minute of his stay.

 The activities in this section are based on the following sample texts.

Text 1: The Bicycle

Bicycles became popular toward the end of the 19th century. They did not cost much, and they did not take up a lot of space. For this reason, more and more people bought them.

Soon, there were bicycle clubs in many cities. On weekends and holidays members would ride to other towns or to the country for picnics. The only difficulty was the roads. They were very bad, and they took a great deal of the pleasure out of riding. The bicycle clubs therefore united to form a "Good Road Movement." Its members talked to people in the government all over the country. They asked for better roads for their bicycles, and little by little, the roads became better.

Text 2: Ancient Roads

The greatest road builders of the ancient world were the Romans. Some of the roads they built are still in use. However, the first roads were not made by people; they were made by animals. Animals make tracks through forests and jungles to get to their drinking places. When people first began to travel, they used these tracks. But, when people began to trade with one another, better roads became important. These roads were not built. They were tracks and trails that became better as more people traveled through them.

When the first pyramids were built in Egypt more than 3000 years ago, people needed real roads to move the huge stones for the pyramids. The first paved roads, made of polished stone, were then built.

Old paved roads that were built at around the same time were also found in Crete. These were also built to help people move building materials from one place to another.

 WHILE READING Find the sentence in the following passage that does not belong.

1. Which sentence does not belong in the text?

2. Use information from the text to justify your answer.

The Bicycle

Bicycles became popular toward the end of the 19th century. They did not cost much, and they did not take up a lot of space. For this reason, more and more people bought them.

Soon, there were bicycle clubs in many cities. On weekends and holidays members would ride to other towns or to the country for picnics. The only difficulty was the roads. They were very bad, and they took a great deal of the pleasure out of riding. These roads were built to help people move building materials from one place to another. The bicycle clubs therefore united to form a "Good Road Movement." Its members talked to people in the government all over the country. They asked for better roads for their bicycles, and little by little, the roads became better.

SAMPLE ACTIVITY **Find the Missing Sentence**
Ancient Roads

A. The greatest road builders of the ancient world were the Romans.
Some of the roads that they built are still in use. However, the first
roads were not made by people; they were made by animals.
Animals make tracks through forests and jungles to get to their
drinking place. _____
But, when people began to trade with one another, better roads
became important. These roads were not built. They were tracks
and trails that became better as more people traveled through
them.

B. When the first pyramids were built in Egypt more than 3000 years
ago, people needed real roads. _____
_____.
The first paved roads, made of polished stone, were then built.

C. Old paved roads that were built at around the same time were
also found in Crete. These were also built to help people move
building materials from one place to another.

 **POST READING TESTING**

The missing sentence in paragraph A is:

    1. When people first began to travel, they used these tracks.

    2. The first paved roads, made of polished stone, were then
       built.

    3. These were also built to help people move building materi-
       als from one place to another.

The missing sentence in paragraph B is:

    1. These were also built to help people move building materi-
       als from one place to another.

    2. Roads were needed to move the huge stones for the pyra-
       mids.

    3. Old paved roads that were built at around the same time
       were also found in Crete.

"Unscrambling"
Two Texts

1. Take two texts and "mix" their sentences, but keep the original
sequence of each. This mixing can be easily done on a word
processor, by moving the first sentence of story 2 to the beginning of story 1, and so on. Have students mark sentences that
belong to one text only (on paper), or separate the texts (on the
word processor). They should note key words, ideas, and other
cohesion markers that led them to the identification of the text.
When they finish marking, they will have two texts, in sequence,
one marked, the other unmarked. If they use a word processor,
they can read each text separately.

The following are two texts in one. Text 1 is called "The Bicycle" and
Text 2, "Ancient Roads." Mark all the sentences that belong to Text 1.

Bicycles became popular toward the end of the 19th century. The
greatest road builders of the ancient world were the Romans. Some
of the roads they built are still in use. They did not cost much, and
they did not take up a lot of space. For this reason, more and more
people bought them. However, the first roads were not made by
people; they were made by animals. Animals make tracks through
forests and jungles to get to their drinking places. Soon, there were
bicycle clubs in many cities. On weekends and holidays members
would ride to other towns or to the country for picnics. The only difficulty was the roads. When people first began to travel, they used
these tracks. But, when people began to trade with one another,
better roads became important. They were very bad, and they took
a great deal of the pleasure out of riding. The bicycle clubs therefore
united to form a "Good Road Movement." These roads were not
built. Its members talked to people in the government all over the
country. They were tracks and trails that became better as more
people traveled through them. They asked for better roads for their
bicycles, and little by little, the roads became better. When the first
pyramids were built in Egypt more than 3000 years ago, people

needed real roads to move the huge stones for the pyramids. The first paved roads, made of polished stone, were then built. Old paved roads that were built at around the same time were also found in Crete. These were also built to help people move building materials from one place to another.

2. Type two texts, one sentence at a time. Cut the sentences up and give each student an envelope containing the sentences from both texts. Students should separate the texts first, and then sequence each.

3. Use the same procedure as in 1 above, but this time, scramble the sentences and do not follow sequence.

▶▶▶ INSIGHTS ◀◀◀

To unscramble two texts students have to use the following skills:

▶ Make associations through the comprehension of factual information and through inferences.

▶ Discriminate and classify by topic.

▶ Become aware of and focus on connectors and other contextual clues.

▶ Become aware of and focus on generalizations and support, references, and definite and indefinite articles.

For students, tasks 2 and 3 are more demanding than 1. They require discrimination and classification skills based on contextual clues, logical sequencing, and attention to backward and forward reference, to definite and indefinite articles, to redundancies and to generalizations and supporting material.

Task 2 is technically easier than 3. Students have the option to move the sentences around and sample sequence before making final decisions.

Recognizing Contradictions

a. The doctor recommended heat. Heat would be the best cure: hot baths, an electric blanket, hot drinks, sun baths. Edna didn't mind doing what the doctor said. She had to remember to avoid the things that he said would be bad for her: cold drinks, ice cream, cold air conditioned rooms, hot showers, and swimming pools.

b. Juancito was a big penguin. He was very strong and had a healthy appetite. Every day Grandpa had to buy fresh fish for him, but he refused to eat it. I got very worried. How long could he live without food?

c. How often can people go to the movies? Some like to go every week or even every day. The problem is that there aren't so many new movies, so they end up going to the same movies more than once. This is fine, because it's always fun to see a new movie.

▶▶▶ INSIGHTS ◀◀◀

By looking for the contradictions in the stories students read closely and look for inconsistencies. This exercise may be followed up by a discussion in which students have to explain what is "wrong," contradictory, or illogical and/or by a writing session in which they either prepare contradictory passages for their classmates, write jokes which are based on a contradiction, or correct the contradictory passages presented.

CAUSE AND EFFECT

In order to develop the recognition of cause-effect relations, teach your students to focus their attention on connectors signaling cause-effect (e.g., *because, therefore, as a result, consequently*).

Also teach implicit cause-effect relationships (where no connector is used) to develop logical thinking processes that are conducive to better reading comprehension.

DISCOURSE MARKERS THAT SIGNAL CAUSE-EFFECT RELATIONSHIPS

> so, then, hence, therefore, consequently, because of this, for this reason, on account of this, as a result, in consequence, for, because, it follows, on this basis, arising out of this, then, that's why, for, since, due to, thanks to, owing to, with this in mind.

Types of activities used to teach cause-effect relations:

- multiple choice cloze (connectors)
- open cloze
- multiple choice (clauses or phrases of cause or effect)
- find the cause (why questions)
- find the effect (so...)
- match causes and effects

 **Introductory Activities**

Move the second half of the sentence into place in order to make acceptable sentences.

> She must be in a hurry because …
> She can't know this area very well because …
> She can't have been gone for long because …
> She must have been on holiday because …
> She must be working very hard because …

SCRAMBLED ENDS: she's got a suntan. she's looking at a map. she's looking very tired. the room's still warm. she's walking very fast.

Camouflage

One of Shakespeare's plays, Macbeth, tells a story of camouflage. Macbeth thought that he would not be killed in battle because an old prophecy said that he could not be killed "Till Birnam forest come to Dunsinane." Macbeth, knowing that trees cannot walk, felt safe. But he was not. An enemy army marched through Birnam woods. To camouflage himself, each soldier cut down a small tree and held it in front of him. The trees of Birnam wood really seemed to march to Dunsinane, and Macbeth was killed.

---

a. Complete the following sentences according to the passage.

> 1. Macbeth thought he could not be killed because …
> 2. As a result of the prophecy, Macbeth thought …
> 3. Macbeth felt safe because …
> 4. As he knew that trees cannot walk, Macbeth …
> 5. Each soldier cut down a small tree so that …
> 6. Each soldier held a small tree in front of him because …
> 7. Macbeth was killed because he believed …

b. Fill in the missing information in the table according to the information in the passage.

CAUSE	EFFECT
	Macbeth thought he could not be killed.
	Macbeth felt safe.
The soldiers marched with trees in their hands.	
	Macbeth was killed.

 ►►► INSIGHTS ◄◄◄

These activities introduce cause-effect relations in simple sentences that contain an explicit marker. Explicitness makes them easy to comprehend. Activity *b* is based on *a* and separates causes from effects.

 A Chain of Causes

Make your students aware of the two possible ways of looking at causes and effects:. You feel hot; therefore, you turn the fan on. Or: You turn on the fan because you feel hot.

In the following list, each sentence is both the effect or result of the previous sentence, and the cause of the following sentence. What is the cause? What is the effect?

> You feel hot.
> You decide to turn the electric fan on.
> You plug the wire into the socket and click the switch on.
> Electricity passes through the switch and into the engine of the fan.
> The engine starts operating.
> The blades of the electric fan begin to rotate.
> The air around you moves.
> Your skin dries up.
> You feel cooler.

Use the above list to write sentences that contain causes and effects. The following expressions can help you: **because, the reason is, as, the effect is, since, therefore, for, as a result, accordingly, consequently, so.**

 Matching Causes and Effects

The purpose of this activity is to distinguish the part of the sentence which is the cause from that which is the effect.

Match the two parts of the sentence. Make sure that the two parts make sense together.

What happened (effect)	Why it happened (cause)
1. He failed his test.	___ It began to rain.
2. She was able to do it.	___ They planned the party well.
3. He got wet.	___ I helped her do the work.
4. They had a wonderful time.	___ He didn't study.
5. John ran quickly.	___ She stepped in a mud puddle.
6. Rena had to change clothes.	___ He is a punctual person.
7. We eat a lot of chocolate.	___ We didn't do our homework.
8. The teacher was angry.	___ It was very hot.
9. I took off my coat.	___ He was in a hurry.
10. My friend came early.	___ We love sweets.

Now combine the two sentences into one, using **because, therefore,** or **so.** For example:

> It began to rain, so he got wet.
> He got wet because it began to rain.

SAMPLE ACTIVITY — Finding Multiple Causes and Effects

1. Prepare cards. Each card has a statement.

2. Put the students into small groups of 4 or 5. Each group gets a card.

3. Ask the students to discuss the statement and to find as many causes and effects as possible.

4. One student of the group writes down the causes and effects.

5. Each group then reads out its card and presents the causes and effects to the rest of the class. In the oral presentation students should use connectors such as *because* and *therefore*.

Example of card: "TV IS MORE POPULAR THAN READING"

Examples of what students may find

Causes

1. because TV has all kinds of interesting programs
2. because it is easier to watch a program than read

Effects

1. Therefore, people don't read much any more.
2. So there are fewer bookstores.

Other suggestions for cards

1. Exams drive students crazy.
2. Traffic accidents cannot be prevented.
3. Pop music stars are teenage heroes.
4. Serving in the army is educational.
5. Parents don't really understand their children.

The Week

The week didn't always have seven days. The ancient Greeks used a ten-day week, the Romans had eight days of market and one day of rest.

There are a couple of reasons why seven days seemed reasonable. The moon goes through four phases in a month: from new moon to half moon and from half moon to full moon. Each phase takes a little more than seven days. The ancient Babylonians noticed this, and used a seven-day division.

Another reason is the religious reason. The Book of Genesis tells about the seventh day as a day of rest, the Sabbath. This seven-day unit of time was adopted by the Jewish people and spread by them to the rest of the world.

There have been attempts to change the week from time to time. Some of them were important in history. In 1929 the government of the then-Soviet Union decided to have four days of work and one day of rest. The days had colors instead of names. All workers were assigned a color that told them which was their day of rest. This system was used so that all stores and factories could be open all the time.

Things got confusing. Special arrangements had to be made for families to have a day off together, and for friends to visit each other. Also, all people who had jobs that included working with other countries had to use the regular seven-day week. As a result, the country went back to using the seven-day week in 1940.

As an introductory activity, prepare WHY questions:

Sample questions:

>Why did the Babylonians decide to have a seven-day week?
>
>Why did the Jewish people use a seven-day week?
>
>Why did the Soviet Union change the week?
>
>Why did this cause confusion?
>
>Why did families have to make special arrangements?

Introduce the notion of multiple causes. Show that for most decisions taken by people and for most events there are usually a number of causes. Use the above passage to demonstrate.

Examples of multiple causes:

The week has seven days because of
- the phases of the moon.
- the story of Creation in the Book of Genesis.
- tradition and habit.

The Soviet attempt to change the week failed because of
- the confusion it brought about.
- the impossibility of friends and family to spend their weekends together.
- foreign trade.

Demonstrate to your learners that just as there are multiple causes, there are also multiple effects.

Examples of multiple effects:

The result of the changes introduced in the Soviet calendar were
- factories could stay open all the time.
- stores stayed open all the time.
- foreign trade suffered.
- families could not meet together on weekends.

Multiple causes and effects: The following are suggestions for discussion. Use them as awareness activities for working with multiple causes and effects in appropriate texts.

Possible topics for multiple causes:
- Why do people cheat on tests?
- What are the causes of unemployment? Inflation?
- What were the causes of the French Revolution? The Second World War?

Possible topics for multiple effects:
The Effects of Space Travel:
- A new science was born.
- New foods were created.
- New jobs were created.
- New industries were developed.
- Our knowledge grew.
- Communications around the world developed.

Other topics:
The effects of
- better nutrition, better medical care.
- highway developments, cheaper cars.
- the development of the micro-computer.
- terrorism.
- the changes in women's status.
- free education.
- smoking.

Organizing Causes and Effects

HARRIET BEECHER STOWE
THE LITTLE WOMAN WHOSE BOOK MADE A GREAT WAR

Until the end of the Civil War, in 1865, many Blacks in the United States were slaves. They were bought and sold, and they had no rights. Their owners could do anything to them, even kill them.

Slaveholders were common in the southern states. In the South, many workers were needed to work in the large cotton fields. In the North, slaves were not needed, because most farmers had small farms and didn't grow cotton. The northern states passed laws against slavery. The southern states refused to give up slavery.

Harriet Beecher Stowe was born in 1811. As a young girl, Harriet often saw the houses of the poor black slaves. Their poverty and hard life made her sad.

Harriet had always wanted to write. At the age of 22 she won first prize in a literary contest. But then, she got married and had seven children, so she was too busy to write.

For many years Harriet lived near a slave-holding community. She saw many run-away slaves, visited their homes and learned all about their life in the South. She helped slaves run away from their masters. The injustice of slavery made her very angry. She decided to write a book to show people how terrible slavery was.

In 1850, Harriet wrote the story of "Uncle Tom's Cabin" for an antislavery newspaper. The story became very popular. It was published in book form in 1852. Five thousand copies were sold in one week, more than a million copies in one year.

The book was translated into 23 languages in its first year. Harriet became very famous. Thousands of letters were sent to her. Half a million British women signed a letter of thanks to her. In many countries people started collecting money to help American slaves.

Harriet often said that she didn't really write the book. She said, "God dictated the story to me. I just took the words down."

Uncle Tom's Cabin showed many people how wrong slavery was. Some slave owners fought against the book. Other slave owners began to free their slaves. Many people said Harriet was lying and that slavery wasn't so terrible.

A few years later, the American Civil War began. It was a terrible war. Brother fought against brother. When the war ended, the slaves were freed. Many people believe that *Uncle Tom's Cabin* was one the causes of the Civil War. After the war, Harriet met the President of the United States, Abraham Lincoln. Lincoln looked at the small woman and said, "So you are the little woman whose book made a great war ... "

POST READING

1. Change the order of the sentences so they make sense—first the cause, then the effect.

1. ☐ They had many slaves.
   ☐ In the South there were large cotton fields.
   ☐ They needed many workers.

2. ☐ In the North they had small farms.
   ☐ They passed a law against slavery.
   ☐ They didn't need slaves.

3. ☐ Harriet had seven children.
   ☐ Harriet was busy.
   ☐ Harriet didn't have time to write.

4. ☐ Five thousand copies of the book were sold in a week.
   ☐ *Uncle Tom's Cabin* became a very popular story.
   ☐ The book was translated into 23 languages.
   ☐ Harriet received letters from all over the world.

5. ☐ People started collecting money to help slaves.
   ☐ People were moved by the story.

6. ☐ The Civil War started.
   ☐ Many people were against slavery.

7. ☐ The slaves were freed.
   ☐ The North won the war.

2. Combine the sentences in each group two ways:

a. In the order they appear.
b. In the order you found in 1.
Use connecting words that show cause and effect, and use pronouns when necessary.
   The following words will help you:
   because, therefore, so, the reason was, as a result, the cause was

Example:
In the South there were large cotton fields.
People needed many workers.
People had many slaves.

In the South there were large cotton fields, so they needed many workers. As a result, they had many slaves. [48]

 Extracting Causes and Effects from Text

There are many opinions and theories that try to explain the causes and results of global warming. The text that follows explains three of them.

IS GLOBAL WARMING A REAL DANGER?

1 One optimistic theory is based on the behavior of clouds. Warming causes more evaporation. As a result, clouds become denser. A dense cloud reflects more sunlight back to space and less sunlight to the Earth. Therefore, in the future, less solar energy will reach the ground, and warming will not be so great.

2 Another theory explains why coastal cities aren't in danger. This theory is based on the idea that much of the evaporated ocean water will fall back to the ground as snow. This snow will build up in the Antarctic in the form of ice. If this trend continues, there will be more ice in the Antarctic and less water in the oceans. The sea level won't rise; it will drop!

3 An important climatologist from the former Soviet Union, Mikhail Bodiko, was the first scientist to predict the greenhouse effect. His predictions are quite optimistic. He believes that the warming up of the globe will have a positive effect on humanity. He thinks that the warming up of the climate will result in more and better crops everywhere.

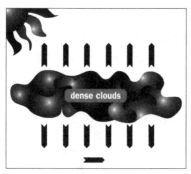

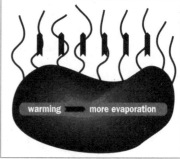

Fill in the missing words according to Paragraph 1.
Warming will not be so great because ...

1. If there is _____ warming, there will be greater evaporation.
2. If there is great evaporation, clouds will _____ denser.
3. If clouds become denser, they will reflect _____ sunlight back to space.
4. If more sunlight is reflected back to space, less solar _____ will reach the ground.
5. If less solar energy reaches the ground, warming will _____ be so great.

Match the causes and the effects according to paragraph 2.

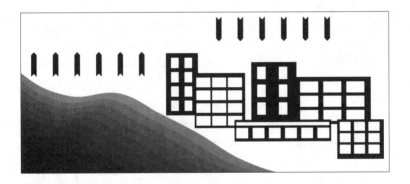

Coastal cities aren't in danger because ...

1. If there is more heat,
2. If there is a lot of evaporation,
3. If there is more snow,

4. If this trend continues,

a. the sea level will drop.
b. the ocean will evaporate more quickly.
c. it will build up in the Antarctic in the form of ice.
d. there will be more ice in the Antarctic and less water in the oceans. [49]

REFERENCES: ANAPHORA
AND CATAPHORA

The use of a reference word (or words) as a substitute for a word or a whole idea preceding (anaphora) or following it (cataphora) is very often confusing to the SL/FL student. Directing the reader's attention to these reference words aids his/her comprehension and establishes the proper connections and associations.

The recognition and comprehension of the logical textual relations created by references requires textual associations and chaining of ideas. These relationships help make the text cohesive, and as a result, coherent to the reader.

To be able to identify the referents (what the references refer to), the following are necessary:

▶ The comprehension of the referent: If the reference word refers to something which is meaningless to the reader, making the association may be impossible.

▶ Background knowledge about the topic: e.g. A text dealing with astrophysics may require areas of knowledge the reader does not have at his/her disposal. As a result, comprehension may fail.

▶ Awareness of the nature of the participants (characters or concepts) in the text: e.g. Sam, Susan, and Bill decided to go shopping, but at the last minute, she decided to go riding instead. To understand that "she" refers to Susan, the reader must be aware of the fact that Susan is the only girl in the text.

▶ Syntactic knowledge allowing the recognition of various relationships, such as subject and predicate in the text.

The recognition and the use of references demand skills which may prove difficult to the SL/FL learner. Speakers of other languages will find the reference system in English difficult if English contains fewer morphological clues than their first language. Many languages mark the verb and the adjective for gender and number, while English marks the verb partially for number only (third person singular) and does not mark the adjective at all.

Point out to your students that

▶ The reference and the referent are not always within the same sentence. They may actually be quite far from each other.

▶ The same word or words may be referred to a number of times and by using various types of references. The more important the character or event is, the more it is referred to in the text.

▶ The chaining of references and referents contributes to the cohesion of texts.

Awareness of the Function of Reference Words

Replace the **boldfaced** words with the words to which they refer. The first paragraph is done as an example.

I lose so many things that I'm sure **they (things)** just get up and walk away. I am jealous of people who are so orderly that they never lose anything. I hate comparing myself to **them (orderly people)**.

Pens and pencils are never there when I need **them**. I try to keep a pen near the telephone so that I will use it when the phone rings. But it is never **there** when I need it.

The situation was getting so bad that I decided to do something about it. I bought a large cupboard with a number of shelves. I then put ten boxes on **them**. I put a label on each box: **one** I labeled *Pens and Pencils*, **another** I labelled *Tools*, **another** *Needles and Pins*. I also bought an address book and put it in the corner of the cupboard. Before **this** I always lost all the addresses and phone numbers I needed. Now I felt very proud of myself.

But things did not change. Pens began to disappear, and one day, I found my hammer under the bed. There was only one solution. I locked the cupboard and put the key on top of **it**. The cupboard was always locked and I was the only one who knew where the key was. Then I lost **it**.

▶▶▶ INSIGHTS ◀◀◀

Have students read the text with the reconstructed references aloud. Help them realize that a text that contains no references is very redundant. That is, elements are repeated again and again, and the flow of the text is not as smooth as it could be. The style is "heavy" and reading it may become quite tedious.

Read the text and answer the multiple choice questions.

> ### APPOINTMENT IN SAMARRA
> **Somerset Maugham**
>
> There was a merchant in Baghdad who sent **(1) his** servant to market to buy provisions, and in a little while the servant came back, white and trembling, and said, "Master, just now when I was in the market-place, **(2) I** was jostled by a woman in the crowd and when I turned, I saw it was Death that jostled me. **(3) She** looked at me and made a threatening gesture. Please lend me **(4) your** horse and I will ride away from this city and avoid my fate. I will go to Samarra and there Death will not find me."
>
> The merchant lent him his horse, and the servant mounted **(5) it,** and he dug his spurs into **(6) its** flanks and as fast as the horse could gallop he went.
>
> Then the merchant went down to the market-place and **(7) he** saw Death standing in the crowd and he came to Death and said, "Why did **(8) you** make a threatening gesture to my servant when you saw him this morning?" "That was not a threatening gesture," Death said."It was only a start of surprise. I was astonished to see him in Baghdad, for I had an appointment with **(9) him** tonight in Samarra."

**POST
READING**

1. **his** refers to
    a. the servant
    b. the merchant
    c. the master
    d. the market

2. **I** refers to
    a. the servant
    b. the merchant
    c. the master
    d. the market

3. **She** refers to
    a. the servant
    b. the merchant
    c. Death
    d. the market

4. **your** refers to
   a. the servant
   b. the horse
   c. the woman
   d. the merchant

5. **it** refers to
   a. the master
   b. the merchant
   c. the woman
   d. the horse

6. **its** refers to
   a. the merchant
   b. death
   c. the horse
   d. Samarra

7. **he** refers to
   a. Death
   b. the servant
   c. the merchant
   d. the horse

8. **you** refers to
   a. Death
   b. the servant
   c. the merchant
   d. the horse

9. **him** refers to
   a. Death
   b. the servant
   c. the merchant
   d. the horse

▶▶▶ INSIGHTS ◀◀◀

The activity is easy, as students have only four options to choose from. Moreover, they can use grammatical clues to narrow down the choices from four to three or two. For example,

> what does the word **his** refer to?
> a. Dr. Watson and Sherlock Holmes
> b. Mrs. Smith
> c. Dr. Watson
> d. The case

In this question, if students realize that **his** is masculine, singular, they can immediately rule out options **a** and **b**. By recognizing the pronoun as referring to a human subject, they can rule out **d**.

Notice that this activity enhances awareness of grammar more than actual reading comprehension. It is only when grammatical information fails to help, that students need to refer back to the text. Consequently, we suggest the following:

▶ More able students may skip this stage.
▶ Less able students may benefit from doing this activity first, but they should eventually move on to other activities in order to focus on textual comprehension (as opposed to sentence or word comprehension).

Find the Connection

You may use the text on page 175 or any other text. In this activity the reference word is in boldface, and students find and mark the referent. The fact that the whole text is there for students to work with allows them adequate time to recognize textual connections and understand how ideas are chained in the entire text.

▶▶▶ INSIGHTS ◀◀◀

This is a completely open activity, as the number of choices available to the reader is as large as the number of phrases in the text. For this reason, it is more demanding than the multiple-choice activity.

 ## Recognizing Multiple References

Read the text and answer the questions that follow.

A Hole in the Sky

Many people are worried because the ozone layer which surrounds the Earth is being destroyed. The ozone layer is very thin. It surrounds the planet at about 20 kilometers above Earth.

This thin layer is very important. It protects us from the sun's ultraviolet radiation, which can cause skin cancer and disturb the growth of animals and plants. The ozone layer is decreasing by 1% to 3% a year.

CFC is the short name for chemicals called chlorofluorocarbons. These chemicals have many uses. They cool refrigerators and air conditioners. They are used to clean electronic parts. They are used in sprays such as deodorants and for making throw-away dishes and keeping the temperature in houses constant.

CFCs were developed in 1930. They have no smell. They don't burn, and they aren't poisonous. Therefore, at that time scientists thought they were the perfect chemicals.

It is true that CFCs are very useful. However, when they reach the stratosphere, they become dangerous. Ozone has three oxygen atoms. When CFC atoms meet the ozone atoms, they remove one of the oxygen atoms from the ozone molecule, and the ozone is destroyed.

In 1985, some British scientists noticed a "hole" in the ozone layer over Antarctica. This hole grows larger and larger every winter, and it disappears when the winds change during the summer. In 1988 it was larger than the whole United States.

At first, scientists were not sure whether the loss of ozone was caused by CFCs. In 1988, they found that the hole was a direct result of the use of CFCs. Many scientists believed that the hole would stay over Antarctica, but they were wrong. Other smaller holes were observed over the Arctic, Norway, and Switzerland. Today, we know that the ozone layer is decreasing by more than 1% every year. Citizens in many countries are worried about this decrease in the ozone layer. They are working to pass laws which forbid the use of products that contain CFCs. Some countries have already passed such laws to protect our planet.

 POST READING Which two references do not refer to CFCs?

1. **These chemicals** have many uses.
2. **They** cool refrigerators and air conditioners.
3. **They** are used to clean electronic parts.
4. **They** are used in sprays such as deodorants.
5. **They** don't burn, and they aren't poisonous.
6. **They** were wrong.
7. **They** are working to pass laws which forbid the use of CFCs.

What is "it" in the following sentences?

1. **It** surrounds the planet at about 20 kilometers above Earth.
2. **It** protects us from ultraviolet radiation from the sun.
3. **It** disappears when the winds change during the summer.

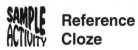 **Reference Cloze**

In this activity, the referent is in boldface, and the reference words are missing. Students must decide what the reference word is.

There was **a merchant** in Baghdad who sent _____ servant to market to buy provisions, and in a little while **the servant** came back, white and trembling, and said, "**Master**, just now when I was in the market-place, _____ was jostled by a woman in the crowd and when I turned, I saw it was **Death** that jostled me. _____ looked at me and made a threatening gesture. Please lend me _____ horse and I will ride away from this city and avoid my fate. I will go to Samarra and there Death will not find me." [50]

▶▶▶ INSIGHTS ◀◀◀

This activity demands production rather than mere recognition. This type of cloze activity requires close reading and comprehension beyond the sentence. It draws students' attention to the chaining of ideas and to the fact that references and referents are not always close to one another.

Read this story.

It is about an animal. Try to guess what animal it's about.

JUANCITO
by J. Schurman

He was walking along the sea. It was a beautiful winter day, and he loved watching the fishermen pull out their nets. He saw a crowd and walked faster; he was curious to know what they were looking at. It was caught in the fishermen's net. They pulled it free, but it was covered with tar and couldn't move.

He wanted to take it home with him. He would clean it and keep it for his three-year-old grandson, Jimmy. The fishermen agreed. They didn't know what to do with it. He took it home with him and patiently cleaned it. It seemed grateful. It seemed to understand that grandfather really cared about it. Grandfather bought some fresh fish—someone told him that it ate fresh fish. Then he brought his grandson to see the new pet.

Jimmy was amazed! He couldn't believe what was on his grandfather's terrace! It was beautiful, and it had a very strong beak. Jimmy called it Juancito. He went to his grandfather's house to visit Juancito every afternoon and Juancito soon learned to come when he heard his name. He ate large amounts of fish and grew bigger and fatter every day. Jimmy came to visit him every day. He felt that Juancito was his. They were real friends.

One day Jimmy's grandfather told Jimmy that he couldn't take care of it anymore. He had to buy large amounts of fish every day. He had to clean the terrace several times a day. Keeping Juancito was too difficult. "Jimmy," grandfather said, "Juancito will be much happi-

---

er at the zoo. Here, he is all alone." Jimmy couldn't believe what grandfather was saying. "Juancito is mine!" he said. Grandfather shook his head sadly. "I can't take care of him here," he said. "I'll take you to the zoo as often as possible." Jimmy tried hard not to cry. They both put Juancito into the car and took him to the zoo. Juancito dived into the water and joined the others.

A month later, grandfather and Jimmy went to the zoo. Jimmy was excited, but grandfather told him not to expect too much. "Juancito might not recognize you," Grandfather said. They came close to a small lake. They couldn't tell which one was Juancito. Jimmy called out in a thin voice "Juancito, here Juancito." The people around couldn't believe their eyes. Suddenly they saw him walk away from the others towards the old man and the child. Jimmy patted him on the head. Juancito did remember him!

POST READING

"He" in the first paragraph is _____.

Juancito is a _____.

If you don't know, fill in the following blanks to help you.

It naturally lives in the _____, but it is not a _____.

It can _____, and it can also _____.

It has a strong _____; therefore, it must be a _____. [51]

▶▶▶ INSIGHTS ◀◀◀

This activity demands inferencing as well as close reading to allow for the recognition of the proper references. Help students realize that the "mysterious" animal is first referred to as "it" and later as "he." This change can be explained by the fact that the penguin becomes closer to the child and is therefore personified.

LOGICAL AND CHRONOLOGICAL SEQUENCING

The awareness of logical and chronological sequencing helps readers understand the development of events in the order in which they occurred. It also allows them to know what the "ideal" order of events should be.

DISCOURSE MARKERS THAT SIGNAL LOGICAL AND CHRONOLOGICAL SEQUENCE

> again, another, also, before that, in addition, first, firstly, first of all, first... then, at first... in the end, first... next... finally, for one thing, further, furthermore, meanwhile, moreover, next, on another occasion, previously, secondly, the third reason, other, last of all, finally, a final reason.

Note: Many sequencing activities are best done on a word processor. When you are working with a word processor, it is easy to move things around so that the final product is a logically or chronologically organized passage rather than a list of numbered sentences.

 ## Sequencing as Pre-Reading

1 The following are events from the story you are going to read.[52]

In each group, one sentence is in the wrong place.
Which one? Where does it belong?

1. It was a familiar voice.
2. She didn't know anybody, and no one knew her.
3. Then she heard a voice behind her.
4. She knew she had heard it before.
5. She automatically turned around.

1. Peggy quickly took her tray.
2. She paid and looked for an empty table.
3. The lady behind her got her tray.
4. The lady agreed.
5. The lady looked around and spotted an empty table.
6. She walked towards the table, and Peggy followed behind.
7. Peggy asked if she could join her at the table.
8. Peggy sat down to eat.

2 Guess

1. Where does the story take place?
2. Whose voice did Peggy hear?
3. Who is the lady?

The purpose of the sequencing task is that students organize events logically. When they finish, they will have a brief summary of the main events in the story. They are therefore ready to predict the gist.

 Simple Sequencing Activities

The following paragraphs have been scrambled. Move the sentences into place to make logically or chronologically sequenced paragraphs.

Mary's Weight-Loss Program

She is actually very happy because she has lost ten pounds since she started. So she has decided to start doing exercises. Mary has been dieting for the past few months. However, she has been eating more food lately. For the past week she has been doing physical fitness exercises and hopes to lose more weight than before.

A Busy Schedule

He had many things to do. Finally, he had to see his lawyer. The man was in a hurry. Second, he had promised to get his wife's car fixed. First, he had some errands to run.

Dreams

People sometimes have nightmares. Everyone dreams at night. Other people never remember what they dream. They dream that they are falling or that they are lost. Some people always remember what they dream.

Read the dialogue and then put the following sentences into the correct order.

Going to a Movie

Marty: Let's check the paper to see what's playing.

David: There's a good movie at the Paramount Theater. It starts at 8:00.

Marty: Is it close enough to walk, or should we take a bus?

David: I think we can walk if we start now, and we can buy drinks and chocolate on the way.

Marty: Yes, it's cheaper to buy outside the movie theater. By the way, how long is the movie?

David: According to the time schedule in the newspaper, it lasts till 11.30.

Marty: Wow, that's a long film!

___ The movie ends very late.

___ The boys will buy food on their way to the movie.

___ Marty and David decide to go to a movie.

___ They will walk to the theater.

___ The movie begins at 8:00 p.m.

 WHILE READING Providing Sequence in Stories

Ask students to number the sentences so that the end product is a logical story.

A Good Day's Work

___ He agreed to give the worker three meals and a day's wages.

___ One day a farmer went looking for a man who would do a day's work for him.

___ The poor man ate dinner.

___ The poor man finished eating supper.

___ The farmer wanted him to start work.

___ The poor man said he never worked after supper.

___ The poor man ate a small breakfast.

___ The poor man agreed to work because he was hungry.

___ The poor man ate supper.

Have students compare with the original story. Draw their attention to the **bold** words and how they can help us understand sequence.

A Good Day's Work

A farmer who couldn't do all the farming by himself looked for help. He offered, "I will give three meals and 100 gold coins to anyone who is willing to do a day's work for me."

This offer was accepted by a hungry poor man, who was really more interested in the meals than in the money.

"You can have your breakfast **first**," said the farmer, "and **then** start work." **After** the farmer had given him a very small breakfast, he said "Perhaps you should have your dinner now too. This will save us a lot of time. The poor man agreed and ate the small dinner as well. **When** he had finished, the farmer said "Well, you might as well have your supper too." The poor man replied "I'll try to enjoy another meal." **When** it was over, the farmer said "Now you can do an easy day's work without wasting any time." "No, thank you," said the poor man **as** he got up to leave, "I never work after supper!"

SAMPLE ACTIVITY   Sequencing Game

1. Prepare cards with a sentence or two on each.

Sample 1: How to answer the telephone:
> Listen to the telephone ring.
> Pick up the receiver.
> Listen to the person on the other end.
> Say: Hello. Who is speaking, please?
> Listen again.
> Say: I'm sorry, you've got the wrong number.

Sample 2: How to order a meal:
> You go to a restaurant.
> You find a table.
> You sit down at the table.
> You look at the menu.
> You speak to the waiter.
> You eat and drink.
> You ask for the check.
> You pay.

Sample 3: How to write a letter:
> Yesterday, my friend took some paper and a pen.
> He wrote a letter.
> He folded the letter in three.
> He put the letter into an envelope.
> He wrote the address on the envelope.
> He stuck a stamp on the envelope.
> He sealed the envelope.
> He posted the letter.

Note: Order of sentences is not absolute. Accept variations as long as they make sense.

2. Prepare smaller cards with connectors such as "at the beginning, first, firstly, second, secondly, third, then, after that, when, subsequently, after doing this, when you have finished, the next step is, the final step is, finally, in the end,...."

3. Prepare one envelope for each group of five students. Each envelope contains Instructions to the students, one card per student with a sentence or two, five cards with connectors.

4. Prepare an empty poster entitled: "HOW TO DO IT" and hang it on the wall.

The following is a list of possible topics that can be used in this activity:

> Boiling an egg.
> Lighting a match.
> Peeling an apple.
> Putting on a coat.
> Opening an umbrella.
> Reading a newspaper.
> Finding an address with the aid of a map.
> Buying a pair of jeans.
> Feeding a dog.
> Washing your clothes.
> Making a salad.
> Washing a car.
> Baking a cake.
> Brushing your teeth.
> Getting a haircut.
> Training a dolphin.

Instructions: In this envelope you will find some sentences and some words. Take one sentence each, read it, and make sure you understand it. In your group, combine the sentences and decide on the best order (or sequence). Look at the connecting words. Decide which words to use and where to use them so that you get a paragraph. Copy your paragraph on the poster.

READ THESE LETTERS

Dear Dr. Cohen,

Thank you for your letter to our daughter, Judith. Our children are tall for their age. Now, thanks to your letter, they are not so worried about their height. They understand that their problem isn't serious.

Thank you again for your letter.

Yours truly,
Alfred Andrews

Dear Judy,

Just now, you are tall for your age, but this is very normal. Why are you so worried? Your parents are not very tall. Chances are you will not be very tall. Your friends are not very tall now, but children grow until they are about 18 or 19 years old. Soon, you and your friends will probably be the same height.

Yours,
James Cohen, M.D.
Pediatric Medicine

Dear Dr. Cohen,

I am 13 years old. All my friends are about 5'4" tall, but I am very tall. My height is 5'9". Why am I so tall?

My parents are not very tall. My father is 5'11" and my mother is 5'4" tall. My little sister is also tall for her age. She's already 5'5" tall. I don't want to be too tall.

I am very worried. What can I do?

Yours sincerely,
Judy Andrews

POST READING

Which letter is first?
Which letter is second?
Which letter is third? [53]

▶▶▶ INSIGHTS ◀◀◀

In this activity, in order to decide on the correct sequence, students need to comprehend the letters. Their acquaintance with similar series will facilitate the task.

SAMPLE ACTIVITY **Sequencing Events**

Prepare your students for the activity by discussing the importance of the sentences and the words that provide clues to the desired order. Students should be reminded that more than one sequence is possible in many instances.

 DO YOU REMEMBER
"CINDERELLA?"

The babysitter told Jimmy the story of Cinderella, but she didn't remember the exact story.

In groups, decide on a logical order for the sentences in each part (number the sentences).

There may be more than one possible order!

Part I

☐ The man had a young daughter who was sweet and good.

☐ Once upon a time there was a gentleman who married for the second time.

☐ She had two daughters who were just like her.

☐ His wife was a very, very proud woman.

Part II

☐ They sat in their rooms and watched TV all day long.

☐ She made the young girl work very hard and do all the dirty work around the house.

☐ Her own daughters did not work around the house.

☐ After the wedding, the stepmother began to show how bad she was.

Part III

☐ However, Cinderella was very pretty, much prettier than her two stepsisters.

☐ The poor girl was very patient and did everything the mean stepmother told her to.

☐ After she finished her work, she usually sat by the microwave oven.

- ☐ She did not tell her father about all this.
- ☐ She was always dirty, so the two sisters called her Cinderella.

Part IV

- ☐ He invited all the important people in the town.
- ☐ The king gave a big party for his son.
- ☐ The two sisters were busy; they had to choose pretty clothes to wear.
- ☐ She had to wash and iron their dresses.
- ☐ Cinderella was very busy too.
- ☐ She also did their hair.

Part V

- ☐ The two mean sisters laughed at Cinderella.
- ☐ She wanted to go to the party.
- ☐ Cinderella did not say anything, but she was very sad.

Part VI

- ☐ She took a shower and did her hair.
- ☐ At last, the big day came.
- ☐ Suddenly, a good fairy came to her.
- ☐ She cried and cried.
- ☐ The two sisters went to the king's palace and poor Cinderella stayed home.

Part VII

- ☐ The good fairy called a taxi.
- ☐ "Well," said the good fairy, "let's do something about that."
- ☐ The good fairy said, "Cinderella, do you want to go to the party?"
- ☐ Cinderella brought the phone.
- ☐ Then she said, "Run to the living room and bring me the phone."
- ☐ "Yes!" cried Cinderella.
- ☐ Cinderella said, "But I can't go to the party! I don't have anything to wear!"
- ☐ So the good fairy gave Cinderella a beautiful dress.

Part VIII

☐ Cinderella promised to do that.

☐ Cinderella got into the taxi and waved goodbye.

☐ The good fairy told Cinderella to leave the palace before midnight.

☐ Then she gave her a pair of beautiful silver sandals.

Part IX

☐ Of course Cinderella's stepsisters did not recognize her!

☐ They danced and danced and everybody watched them.

☐ "Ah! How beautiful she is!" thought the prince.

☐ "Ah! How handsome he is!" thought Cinderella.

☐ All the ladies talked about Cinderella's beauty, her dress, and her hair.

☐ When Cinderella walked in, the prince fell in love with her.

Part X

☐ But who was she?

☐ The king's son picked up the sandal.

☐ At a quarter to twelve, Cinderella ran away.

☐ He said that he was in love and wanted to marry the beautiful girl.

☐ One of her silver sandals fell off her foot.

Part XI

☐ The prince put an ad in the paper.

☐ Her stepmother and her sisters were shocked.

☐ She called the palace.

☐ The prince sent a helicopter to get her.

☐ Cinderella and the prince lived happily ever after.

☐ Cinderella saw the ad. [54]

Lost Love!

If you have a left silver sandal, size 7, call the palace toll-free 800 555-1234 and ask for the Prince.

Sequencing a Long Narrative

Suggested procedure: Work with a short story that is not chronologically sequenced. Divide the class into groups. Each group should work on different parts of the story. The whole class should decide on the order of the parts.

▶▶▶ INSIGHTS ◀◀◀

Many stories are written in a sequence that deviates from the real chronological order. If you deal with such a story, discuss the reason for changing the order. You may ask students to recall a film or a book that illustrates this technique. For example, many detective stories and films follow a backward sequence. That is, at the beginning of the story we read about events that culminate a series of events, and then we work our way backwards, to understand what really happened. This sequence makes the reader more involved in the story. The reader has information that one or more of the protagonists lack, and interest arises as to how and when the protagonists will find out what happened.

This type of activity, which demands sequencing on a number of levels, may be accompanied by the completion of a time line. A time line will help groups sequence events chronologically and thus overcome the confusion that may have been caused by the flashbacks in the story.

 Sequencing a Newspaper Page

Photocopy a few pages from a newspaper. Cut them up into single articles. Give a cut-up page to each group. In their groups, students should arrange the articles according to prominence, logical sequence, items that might be of special interest to readers, and items that deserve special attention because of their importance. Each group produces a "newspaper page" which is then compared with the original. Discuss differences and similarities. Groups should justify their organization.

SAMPLE ACTIVITY — Sequencing According to Perceived Prominence

Arrange news items of a certain day or a whole week in descending order — from the most important news item to the least important. Students may need your help. Provide guidelines: discuss the notion of "importance" in newspapers, use actual newspapers to see how prominence is shown, and use the next activities to make students aware of the problems involved.

Individual work:

The student should explain in writing or orally:
> a. What makes each item prominent/not prominent?
> b. What helped him/her decide?

Group work:

> a. What were the individual criteria for making decisions?
> b. Arrive at a group consensus. What are the best criteria for decisions of this type?
> c. Read final decisions. Did you classify the information into themes? (Politics, economics, finance, literature, entertainment, etc.) Would such a classification be helpful? How?
> d. Should the sequence be changed? Decide on a final sequence.

SUMMARIZING

A summary is a systematic condensation or reduction of the information in a text. The factual information, main ideas, and important generalizations are synthesized while the examples, illustrations, and other supporting materials are removed. This process requires a thorough understanding of the material that is being read.

> briefly, to sum up, in conclusion, to conclude, therefore, finally, for these reasons, in short, thus, then, so, consequently, as a result, hence, in summary, last of all, to resume, to point, as I said above, we have seen that, in a word.

 Guided Summaries

The most obvious activity is asking students to summarize a text that they have read. Guidelines should be provided.

▶ Inform students of the number of propositions (ideas) they should include.

▶ Provide guiding questions: *Who? What? Where?* Then, check to see if answers to these questions were included in the summaries produced.

▶ Provide paragraph beginnings.

▶ Provide the first paragraph of the summary.

▶ Provide a model summary based on another text.

▶ Have students locate the main ideas in each paragraph of the original passage, combine them, and evaluate the product as a possible summary.

 Locating examples and other supporting details

Instructions: 1. On paper: mark all examples in color.
2. On a word processor: delete all examples.

Optical Illusions

"Seeing is believing" is a common saying. However, you shouldn't always believe what you see. Sometimes we don't see things as they really are because our eyes can play tricks on us. These tricks are called optical illusions.

Water makes things seem to be where they are not. Light rays from an object under the water bend as they leave the water. This bending causes an illusion. If you aim your fishing line at a fish where it seems to be, you will miss it.

The size of the full moon as it rises is a common optical illusion. When the moon is near the horizon, it appears much larger than it appears when it is high in the sky. Actually, it is not larger. If you photograph the huge moon when it is low near the horizon, chances are that you will be disappointed. In the photograph, the moon will look very small. The moon can fool our eyes, but it cannot fool the camera. This optical illusion was studied by the ancient Greeks, but they were not able to explain it.

Our eyes often fool us when we look at moving things. We may see motion when there isn't any. In a clear sky, the moon appears to be still. But, when it is surrounded by moving clouds, it appears to race across the sky while the clouds seem to stand still. Actually, the opposite is true. We tend to think that large objects stand still while small ones move. Whenever there is movement, we have to decide what's moving and what isn't moving.

In a moving car, it is sometimes hard to tell which car is moving — the car we are in or the one next to us. This illusion also occurs in air travel, especially at night. Pilots learn to trust their instruments rather than their eyes. The first astronauts that landed on the moon faced an even more serious problem. They couldn't trust their eyes to tell them what was far and what was near.

Optical illusions are used by architects, home decorators, and dress designers. Vertical lines on the wall, for example, make a ceiling look higher than it really is, while a horizontal line around the room will make the ceiling look lower. If you are very thin, and you want to look heavier, wear a shirt with horizontal lines. On the other hand, if you want to appear thinner than you really are, wear something with vertical lines. [56]

▶▶▶ INSIGHTS ◀◀◀

To locate examples, students have to identify them on the basis of markers and specific content. If they do this activity on a word processor, they will realize that the text kept its meaning, that it is more abstract and therefore possibly less interesting. They will also see that what is left is a collection of the main ideas.

 A Summary Cloze

SHOULD WE WORRY ABOUT GLOBAL WARMING?
A Scientific Controversy

Most scientists agree that there will be some global warming. However, not all scientists agree about the effects of global warming. For example, some scientists predict that New York City and other coastal cities will eventually be covered by the ocean. Others believe that coastal cities are not in any danger. They don't know exactly what changes will take place or when they will take place.

Scientists also disagree about how much global warming can be expected. Some think that global warm-

---

ENHANCING READING COMPREHENSION

ing may be only half as great as predicted. Others predict that we are heading towards a climatic disaster if the greenhouse gases increase by 1%.

The big fear of environmentalists is that the planet will grow so warm that life will be almost impossible. However, a number of scientists have developed theories that lead to more optimistic predictions. So, what are the effects of greenhouse warming? The answer you get may depend on who you ask.

  Complete the summary.

Most scientists agree that there will be some _____. However, not all scientists agree about the _____ of this phenomenon. Some scientists predict that cities near the _____ will eventually be covered by the ocean. Others don't believe it at all.

Scientists also disagree about how _____ global warming there will be. Some scientists are very pessimistic and think that warming will make life almost _____. Others are more _____ in their predictions.

▶▶▶ INSIGHTS ◀◀◀

A summary cloze is a valuable concluding activity for a text that has been used in class. It can also assess reading comprehension test. This activity is considered especially valuable because it taps many skills and strategies that went into the processing of the text. It reviews main ideas, vocabulary, and factual information that was gathered during reading. It also taps sequencing and all the logical and chronological relations displayed in a particular text.

Note that a summary cloze can be done in a number of ways:

1. as a discourse cloze where no options are provided. This version demands retrieval and production. It is therefore the most difficult version. Note that when checking this version, you should allow for "acceptable" words; that is, words that make sense within the text and do not change the original meaning intended by the author.

2. with a bank of words, including all the words needed with the addition of a number of words from the same text that are inappropriate in context (distractors). This version demands recognition and selection of the appropriate words.

3. with a bank of words, including all and only the words needed. This is the easiest version, for it demands only recognition and discrimination.

All three versions demand reading with comprehension, both the original text and the summary cloze.

The Use of Sequencing in Summarizing

In the activity that follows, students must put paragraphs in a logical sequence and then write a summary of the story that results.

 **Sequencing and Summarizing**

A newspaper editor wants to make sure that a story tells the most important facts first. The first paragraphs have to answer questions such as who the story is about, what happened, where it happened, when, and why. When this information is clear, other details follow.

Re-arrange the following paragraphs so that they make a good newspaper story.

Girl Saves Baby

The local Lifeguards Association has decided to award Shelley a prize for her courageous act.

"I was talking to my friend," said the baby's mother. "I was watching the baby all the time. I cannot understand what happened. I will be thankful to Shelley for the rest of my life."

Shelley was the only one who noticed that the baby fell. Without a moment's hesitation, she jumped into the water, dived, and pulled the baby out. The baby was not hurt.

Shelley, a fourteen-year old girl, became a heroine today by saving a two-year old baby who almost drowned. The baby was crawling around the public swimming pool on Main Street when it suddenly fell into the water.

When we spoke to Shelley, she was excited. "I don't think that I did something special," she said. "I did what I thought was the right thing to do."

▶▶▶ INSIGHTS ◀◀◀

The sequence of the first paragraphs is quite obvious. However, a number of sequences are possible towards the end of the story, depending on what students consider more important– Mother's reaction, Shelley's reaction, the award. Discuss the variations in class.

 POST READING Summarize the newspaper story in one paragraph. Include all the important details in the story.

Note: Go over the summaries. Obviously, you will get a great variety of summaries. Explain that the length and form of a summary will vary according to its purpose. The shortest summary possible is a title or a headline. Discuss this concept with your students. Have them suggest titles and subtitles for a newspaper story.

HEADLINES AS SUMMARIES

The Language of Headlines

A headline is usually concise and to the point. It must appeal to the attitudes and interests of the intended reader. The language of newspaper headlines has a number of features which make it special. The most prominent features are

- Unnecessary words are deleted. There are no articles or auxiliary verbs: "Actor Found Dead" instead of "An Actor Has Been Found Dead."

- Whenever possible, words are abbreviated or shortened: "Doc Freed" instead of "A Doctor Has Been Freed."

- Prepositions are avoided when possible: "London Man Dead" instead of "A Man from London Has Been Found Dead."

- Nouns form groups: "London Drug Case Lawyer Fired" instead of "A Lawyer from London Working On a Drug Case Has Been Fired."

- Tense and Time: As a rule, very few tenses are used.

- Using the simple present tense gives a sense of immediacy: "Actor Dies" (instead of *Died*).

- The simple past tense is rarely used, except to report on reports, such as court cases: "Policeman Fought 3 Gunmen, Court Hears."

- Passive "be" left out: "Workers Checked After Radiation Leak" instead of "Workers Are Checked After Radiation Leak."

- Future: Only the infinitive form is used: "The President to Open Health Center."

- Vocabulary is usually very descriptive and economical: **alert** (warning), **ban** (prohibition), **blaze** (fire), **curb** (restrain)

Working with Newspaper Headlines

1. Each student scans the newspaper for the "clearest" headline of the day. This headline should give the reader a clear idea of what the story is about.

In the following lesson have students sit in groups. Each student reads "his headline." The others in the group try to guess the whole story. The headline that includes the best clues (i.e., most of the information could be guessed) is selected as the "best headline."

2. Distribute some headlines from a current newspaper. Students rewrite the headline as a sentence, adding all the missing words and rewording if necessary. This exercise should be repeated a number of times.

3. In most cases, the "sentence form" of the headline reappears in the main body of the article. Look for articles that display this phenomenon, and ask students to find the sentence which is a paraphrase and expansion of the headline.

4. Distribute articles with no headlines. Keep the headlines. Have students prepare headlines and later compare to the original.

5. Personal headlines: Write a headline about yourself. Use a thick marker and a full page to write. Possible headings: Tired teacher needs rest / Teacher reads papers all night / Teacher needs time / Teacher fails test, etc. Students should be allowed to ask questions about the contents of the article.

Now, students write their own headlines. Encourage them to tell the truth. Walk around the room and provide assistance when necessary. Each student produces a headline and hangs it up. (No names). Students are now allowed to mill around the room to find headlines that interest them. When they go back to their seats, they can ask the writer to identify himself / herself and to give details.

6. Ask students to think of a well-known story. They pretend the story has just happened and produce a newspaper headline for it. Students will come up with amusing headlines. Some examples: Wolf Munches Grandma (Little Red Riding Hood), Prince finds Right Foot (Cinderella), etc. Student reads his/her headlines and the class tries to identify the story.

Dentistry

Our teeth are a very important part of our bodies. They enable us to chew a variety of foods and to pronounce many sounds.

Sometimes our teeth give us trouble. A tooth may ache, get infected, or decay. Specialist doctors who treat teeth are called dentists.

Dentists can treat aching teeth, straighten teeth that are crooked, put an artificial tooth where one was lost, and even make a whole new set of teeth. By taking X-rays they can find any hidden trouble. A very important part of a dentist's work is to teach us how to take care of our teeth and how to prevent trouble in the future.

Dentists today use modern instruments and medicines that dull the pain that used to accompany treatment. When a tooth cannot be saved, they can pull it out with little or no pain.

In early times people probably had much less trouble with their teeth than we do. They exercised their teeth by eating coarse food. This is why dentistry is a rather new profession. There were no real dentists until about 250 years ago, and the first school for dentists was only founded in 1840.

At first, teeth were treated along with other parts of the body. The general practitioners knew how to pull teeth when their medicines failed. These were very peculiar–tortoise blood, garlic, and "sea dragon" bones. Magic was often called on to help cure toothaches.

During the Middle Ages, barbers took over the pulling of teeth. Some of them were so skillful that they grew to be quite famous.

To be a dentist today, however, a person has to study for many years. She must take examinations to receive a license to practice, just as any other doctor.

a. Have students identify the main idea in each paragraph. Notice that in this case it is always the first sentence.

b. Discuss the structure of the paragraph with your students. Make sure they realize that other locations for main ideas are also possible, especially at the end of the paragraph.

c. Divide your class into two. Ask half your students to collect the main ideas and put them together in the format of an outline. The other half will put the sentences together in the form of a summary.

 **►►► INSIGHTS ◄◄◄**

The difference between the two formats should be noted. An outline demands clear divisions and enumerations. Headlines (phrases) rather than whole sentences are used. A summary demands the condensation of main ideas and examples and usually looks like a complete paragraph. The students may have to add connectors.

 ## Text Mapping as Post Reading

Mapping a text results in an organized condensed outline. It provides students with a framework to guide them in their summarizing. Correct completion of the map reflects comprehension.

SKY CITIES

Some American cities have become so huge that a large part of the population live in the suburbs around them. Traveling time has become a real problem for many Americans. Many people travel more than two hours to work. But soon, many Americans may arrive home after traveling less than a mile and a half — that is, a mile and a half upwards.

Some architects in the United States suggest solving the urban problems by building huge skyscrapers. They base their plans on technologies that will protect these buildings in the sky against strong winds, earthquakes, and other natural forces. A number of plans are already under way.

A building called the Houston Tower will have 500 floors and will be over a mile and a half high. It will have 56 elevators that will move at a speed of about 55 mph. The elevators will be like cars that move up and down instead of forward. The parking area below the ground level will have room for 15,000 cars, and the roof will provide landing space for 100 helicopters.

Another sky building is being planned in Chicago, Illinois. The Chicago New World Trade Center will be one of the tallest buildings in the world. Some designers are disappointed that it will be only 2,300 feet high. (Compare to the Empire State Building which is 1,500 feet high, to the New York World Trade Center which is 1,240 feet high, and to the Sears Building in Chicago which is 1,330 feet tall.) This building will have 210 floors and will be divided into seven sub-buildings, 30 floors high each. This special design will solve the problems caused by winds.

These are just two examples. There are a few other plans for huge skyscrapers, but the interesting thing about these buildings is that they will function as cities and not as houses. They will provide the people who live in them with everything they need. The buildings will have apartments, shops, offices, entertainment facilities, service areas, and power stations. The planners of the Houston Tower are even considering a special police force that will take care of problems within this Sky City.

TEXT ORGANIZATION[52]

Complete the chart.

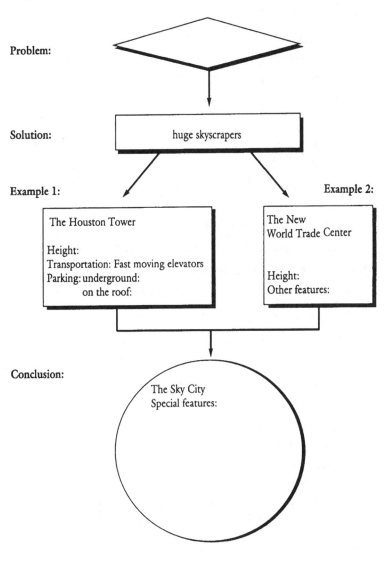

Problem:

Solution: huge skyscrapers

Example 1:

The Houston Tower

Height:
Transportation: Fast moving elevators
Parking: underground:
          on the roof:

Example 2:

The New
World Trade Center

Height:
Other features:

Conclusion:

The Sky City
Special features:

Expanding a Summary to Form a Text

1. Classify the following sentences logically. This exercise will provide you with a minimal summary of a text.

2. Expand the summary to write a full text.

   Facts about whales.

   1. Whales eat plankton and small fish.

   2. Female whales can give birth only once every three years.

   3. Whales begin to reproduce between the ages of ten and thirty.

   4. Some female whales help mother whales take care of their young.

   5. Whales give birth to live young.

   6. Whales use sound for communicating with one another.

   7. The whales' sonar helps them find their way.

   8. Whales have warm blood and breathe air.

   9. Whales have highly developed brains.

   10. Whales use sound as a type of sonar to detect objects.

   11. Today there are very few blue whales left.

   12. Male and female blue whales may not be able to find each other across the oceans.

   13. The blue whale reaches a length of 35 meters and weighs up to 160 tons.

   14. The blue whale is the largest animal known. [53]

▶▶▶ INSIGHTS ◀◀◀

This procedure is the reverse of summarizing. Here students begin with a list, continue with an organized list, and end up with a text.

PUTTING IT ALL TOGETHER: DISCOURSE SKILLS

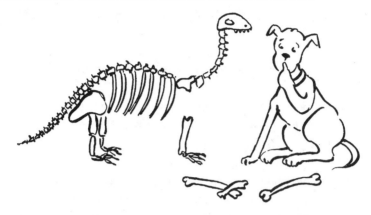

Discourse comprehension is defined as the understanding of an entire text, the elements of cohesion that hold it together, and the overall meaning, concepts, and ideas conveyed. Obviously, there is a close interaction between the reader and the text, which means going beyond the details in any single sentence. When doing activities that demand discourse comprehension, the student simultaneously learns from the intensive exposure to the text, from the process of reading itself, and from the task which demands focus on the global elements as well as from the metalinguistic awareness which is provided by the feedback.

THE CLOZE TASK AS A READING COMPREHENSION ACTIVITY

The cloze task is a language learning or testing activity in which words are systematically deleted from a text. In order to reconstruct the text, students are required to make decisions on the basis of context. In this gap-filling activity, supplying the suitable words is considered evidence of comprehension of the text. However, it has been noted that different types of deletions measure different abilities. In fact, the recovery of function words measures the reader's knowledge of syntax and grammar, while the recovery of other words may measure background (pragmatic) knowledge.

The traditional procedure employed for cloze is the deletion of every nth (e.g. 6th or 7th) word in the text. This procedure is considered a task which taps the students' overall linguistic abilities as well as their world knowledge and cognitive skills. Moreover, this guideline is convenient and easy to prepare. However, recent studies show that the words deleted in such a manner tend to be mostly function words. Their recovery often requires only sentence-level comprehension.

To maximize text comprehension, selected lexical items can be deleted. Each deletion must be carefully weighed and selected depending on the teaching point selected. This type of cloze is usually referred to as a rational cloze. This procedure has a distinct advantage. The teacher may prepare a cloze task which taps preselected categories and thus make the rational cloze relevant to a particular population and for specific strategy emphasis.

Three Kinds of Cloze Procedures

Note: We strongly suggest that you do the following as a student. Experiencing the process of retrieval is important. It will make you aware of the actual mental processes involved. You will realize that contrary to popular beliefs, not every cloze activity involves reading comprehension, although it may be a valuable writing or language activity. Activities 1 and 2 exemplify this issue.

SAMPLE ACTIVITY

1. Guided Creative Writing through Cloze

Fill in each blank with one word.

It is a great experience to go on a ___. I went to the ___ and sat down. For a while, I looked at the ___. Then, I listened to the ___. It was very ____.

The lady next to me was ___. Her eyes were ___ and she had two ___ and another small ___. Later that day, we almost became ___. When we arrived at ___, I felt very ___. I knew that I would always ___ the experience. I knew I would never ___ it.

▶▶▶ INSIGHTS ◀◀◀

The original words which were deleted from this passage are difficult to retrieve. These words are not retrievable because of lack of contextual clues. However, the task is relatively easy. Readers may be able to supply the proper closure on the basis of their world knowledge. The words are constrained syntactically, but not semantically. That is, you know whether you need a noun, a verb, an adjective or an adverb, but you have no way of knowing the meaning needed. Actually, very many words are possible within each blank. The choice of words depends on the reader and not on the context. The decisions made at the initial stage create a context for the "story."

For these reasons, the activity is a structured or guided creative- writing activity rather than a reading activity.

2. Language Cloze

1. Do this cloze as quickly as you can.

> Overheating might destroy or incapacitate ___ target such ___ a missile by any ___ several mechanisms. ___ amount of energy per unit area ___ would have to be delivered to the target in ___ to damage it would depend ___ the mechanism chosen and the vulnerability ___ the target to that mechanism.

2. Cover the cloze passage. Do you remember what the text is about?

Probably not. The reason for this difficulty is that you did not need to comprehend the text in order to do this cloze.

▶▶▶ INSIGHTS ◀◀◀

This cloze task does not demand reading comprehension or familiarity with the topic. Performance depends on familiarity with sentence structure and collocations. Therefore, the better you know the language, the easier it becomes to do this type of cloze. All the deletions can be retrieved within the sentence. That is, you need limited context to make decisions, but you DO NOT need to understand it. There is only one possible answer that will fit each blank, since the decisions are mostly grammar based and not context based. Decisions are made locally, and students can skip from one blank to the other and perform quite well, without reading the whole text.

3. Discourse Cloze

The following cloze task demands that you read the passage carefully and supply the missing words on the basis of your comprehension.

Appointment in Samarra
by W. Somerset Maugham

There was a merchant in Baghdad who sent his servant to market to buy provisions and in a little while the servant came _____, white and trembling, and said, "Master, just now when I was in the _____, I was jostled by a woman in the crowd and when I turned, I saw it was Death that ____ me. She looked at me and made a threatening gesture. Please lend me your horse, and I will run away from this ____ and avoid my ____. I will go to Samarra, and there ____ will not ____ me."

The merchant ____ him his horse, and the ____ mounted it, and as fast as the ____ could gallop he went.

Then the merchant went down to the market-place, and he saw Death standing in the crowd, and he came to Death and said, "Why did you make a ____ gesture to my ____ when you saw him this morning?" "That was ____ a threatening ____," ____ said. "It was only a start of surprise. I was ____ to see him in ____, for I had an ____ with him tonight in ____."

▶▶▶ INSIGHTS ◀◀◀

This cloze task demands reading with comprehension. The words are contextually, semantically, and syntactically constrained. That is, all the deleted words are cohesive in nature and in order to retrieve them, the entire text needs to be comprehended. This results in a real reading comprehension cloze.

How does the recovery of deleted words facilitate the complex reading process? In a discourse cloze, different types of semantic and syntactic words have to be recovered. These words include topic or key words, lexical repetition, summary words, and logical connectors of various sorts. If one's comprehension of the context is effective, the deletions only affect the total comprehension temporarily, as the line of ideas, the global aspect of the text as a total unit is still there. The reader must be able to comprehend the gist in order to make sense of the text.

How to Prepare your own Discourse Cloze

1. Select a text, expository or narrative. It should not be too difficult or too long. Don't use poetry, journalistic materials, recipes, or ads.

2. Analyze your text and locate: repetitions, synonyms, reference words, logical connectors, and summary words. Select your deletions from these categories.

3. Decide on a minimum distance between deletions (at least 6 words).

4. Go over your cloze, do it as a student, and try it out on at least one student before you use it in class. Make sure there are enough contextual clues to allow recovery.

Chapter Eight

▶ ▶

Processes of Evaluation

The evaluation of a text is a high order process. Here, the students are expected not only to read with comprehension but also to read critically. Reading critically implies, among other things, being able to recognize whether the writer is being subjective and is expressing personal opinions, or being objective, using undistorted facts.

The student is also required to differentiate between material approved of by the author and other material which the author tries to refute. Students pay little attention to an author's bias when it matches their own bias. Therefore, encouraging the students to read critically means helping them become aware not only of the author's bias, but of their own.

FACT VS. OPINION

DISCOURSE MARKERS THAT SIGNAL STATEMENTS OF OPINION

> in my opinion, I believe, it is said, it seems, the so-called, it appears, it is my contention, in my view, as a matter of fact, actually, it is my conviction, no doubt, certainly, positively, I am sure, undoubtedly, obviously, surely, one must note that, may, might, should, must, ought to, unfortunately, luckily.

 Introductory Writing Activity

A good activity to demonstrate to your learners how people express their opinion is to let them write a short passage that demands a stated opinion. Ask learners to write about one or any of the following topics. Vary the topics according to your students' interests and level.

1. Write your opinion on any topic about which you have strong feelings. Decide who you are writing to, a newspaper or the school principal and try to be very convincing.

Suggested topics:
- ▶ Watching television
- ▶ Army Service
- ▶ Standardized tests
- ▶ Homework
- ▶ Studying another language
- ▶ A political party
- ▶ The problems of the national economy

2. Find in your own writing words that express your opinion. Look for words and expressions such as **seems, know, believe, appears, feel, like, think, guess, this means, want, should, remember.**

Look for descriptive adjectives such as **great, interesting, boring, easy, fair, important, good, ugly, special, bad, beautiful, effective, best, certain, excellent, sure, difficult, wonderful.**

3. Add more of these words to make your writing more convincing.

4. Exchange papers. Read your classmate's paper. Evaluate its objectivity/subjectivity, and judge how convincing it is.

 ## Distinguishing Fact from Opinion

Mr. and Mrs. Rodriguez are looking at a new house. Read what Mrs. Rodriguez says about the new house and what Mr. Rodriguez says about it. Underline those sentences which express opinion.

Mrs. Rodriguez: This is a beautiful large house.

Mr. Rodriguez: It is only 2000 square feet.

Mrs. Rodriguez: It seems very, very clean, and it has at least two windows in every room.

Mr. Rodriguez: It appears to have a nice view from the living room window. However, this house costs $100,000.00. That seems to be very expensive.

Mrs. Rodriguez: I think it seems reasonable for such a nice house.

Mr. Rodriguez: Well, it does have 4 bedrooms and 3 bathrooms but it still appears to be too small for our family.

Who do you think is more enthusiastic about the house?
Give reasons.

ON THE MOON
Are you ready to take a trip to the moon?
Read this before you decide!!!

There is no water or air on the moon. You'll have to bring your own oxygen and your own water. It is silent on the moon because there is no air. There is no music and there are no sounds. There are no rivers and no lakes. At night, it is very cold. The temperature goes down to -240°F (240 Farenheit degrees below zero), or -151° C. Nights are so cold that without a space suit you turn into ice in a few seconds. During the day the temperature rises to 212°F, or 100°C above zero!!!

What does the moon look like? There are great round holes in the moon. They are called craters. There are more than 30,000 craters on the moon. There are also high mountains. The Leibnitz Mountains, the highest mountains on the moon, are about 26,000 feet, or 8,000 meters high.

On the moon you will weigh 1/6 of what you weigh on earth. If you weigh 110 pounds, or 50 kilos, on the moon you will weigh only 18 pounds, or a little more than 8 kilos. You will be able to jump very high and take very long steps. You will jump higher than an Olympic champion, but you won't be able to take off your space suit. Maybe you won't sleep very well because one day on the moon lasts for two weeks.

A fact is something that can be proved or that everyone will accept as true. If you say, "It's very cold today," you can check the thermometer to prove it.

An opinion is your personal judgment. If you say, "This is a good TV program," other people may disagree with you.

POST READING

Read these statements and decide what they are.
Write F (fact) or O (Opinion).

1. _____ There isn't water on the moon.
2. _____ The moon is very ugly.
3. _____ The weather on the moon is terrible.
4. _____ People will like the moon because it is quiet.
5. _____ In 25 years, people will live on the moon.
6. _____ There are no sounds on the moon.
7. _____ There should be a space station on the moon.
8. _____ There are no rivers and no lakes on the moon.
9. _____ At night, it is very cold on the moon.
10. _____ The temperature goes down to -151°C.
11. _____ There is no reason to learn about the moon.
12. _____ There are many craters on the moon.
13. _____ The Leibnitz Mountains are on the moon.
14. _____ People should visit the Leibnitz Mountains.
15. _____ The moon is a good place for a vacation. [54]

Note: Students should be made aware that although they may agree with a certain opinion, their agreement will not make the opinion into a fact.

 SAMPLE ACTIVITY

Locating Facts and Opinions

Distribute newspaper articles to students. Use some articles from the lead pages and some from the editorial page.

Ask students to find sentences that express opinion and to find as many statements of fact as they can.

Discuss their findings. Which articles contain more facts? Which contain more opinions? How can they tell which is a factual article and which is an opinion article? Which belongs on the lead page or the editorial page?

POINT OF VIEW

To introduce students to the concept of point of view, read a news report or a short story in class, and then ask students to rewrite it from another point of view. Possible points of view include that of:

▶ A character in the story (a person involved in the events)

▶ A person from another country

▶ A visitor from another planet

▶ An item in the story (anything goes: a chair, a flower, and so on)

▶ A five-year-old child

▶ A politician, a scientist, a psychologist, or someone else in a specialized field

Read the students' reports in class. In each case, ask how the story changed. To conclude, discuss how point of view changes details, approach, emphasis, and so on.

Identifying Point of View

THE WORLD IS CHANGING!

| ☐ **Mr. Bond** Baker | ☐ **Mr. Ruiz** Scientist | ☐ **Mr. Nakamura** Salesman |
| ☐ **Mrs. Baree** Sports Teacher | ☐ **Mr. Teva** Cook | ☐ **Mr. Lee** Retired |

Who said what?

Write the correct number under each picture.

1 The world is changing. New things are happening every day. People are going to the moon. They are sending satellites into orbit. Computers are doing all kinds of things. Robots are doing the jobs that people once did. They can work and work and they never get tired! The modern world is exciting!

2 The world is changing. Once people ate plain regular bread! Life was boring. See that supermarket across the street? They sell all kinds of bread. These days people are buying round bread, buns, and baguettes. They are eating sweet bread with pecans and salty bread with onions. The modern world is full of new things. Every meal is a surprise!

3 The world is changing. Look at that young man sitting over there. He looks terrible! What kind of clothes is he wearing? He's wearing tennis shoes instead of shoes. When I was a young man, people knew how to dress! No one buys elegant clothes anymore. What are people going to wear in ten years?

4 The world is changing. The world is getting smaller. People are traveling more and more. We know things about other peoples and we can visit faraway places. But you know, people don't walk anymore. They even take their car, to the supermarket. They don't get enough exercise. They're getting fat and lazy. People are having more and more trouble with their backs. Will the children of the future be able to play football?

5 The world is changing. People are not cooking anymore. They are buying ready-made food. They are using frozen meats and vegetables. They are eating pizzas and hamburgers. They're drinking Cokes and colored juices. They don't remember the taste of homemade food. Ah...my mother...she could cook!

6 The world is changing. People don't like music anymore. They call noise "music"! See my granddaughter, over there? What do you think she's listening to? Noise! That's what she's listening to—noise that is bad for your ears! In a few years, we are all going to be deaf.

POST READING **Find sentences in the text and make two lists.**

Sentences that **praise** the modern world
    1. They are sending satellites into orbit.
    2.
    3.
    4.
    5.
    6.
    7.

Sentences that **criticize** the modern world.
    1. We are all going to be deaf.
    2.
    3.
    4.
    5.
    6.
    7.   55

▶▶▶ INSIGHTS ◀◀◀

In these activities students are made aware of the fact that the writer's point of view has an effect on his/her writing. They learn to recognize point of view.

REFUTATION

A refutation is an argument that attempts to prove another argument wrong. After defining refutation in class, ask students to do the activity that follows. The activity contains several different tasks.

 SAMPLE ACTIVITY Some experts feel that in the computerized world of the future we will not need prisons. They have suggested other forms of punishment. Their ideas are based on modern technology.

Read a report from the year 2027.

NO MORE PRISONS!

Report no.: 225
Date: July 13, 2027
By: Prof. Criminez
Position: Professor of Criminology
To: Criminal Justice Committee

Criminals haven't changed, but our criminal punishment system has greatly improved. Over the centuries, society has used different systems to punish criminals. We have tried putting criminals away in prisons. This punishemnt made them victims of society. We treated the criminal like a terrible disease. We did not forgive, and we did not usually give second chances.

Crime is treated very differently now. The following is a report of the way crime is handled at present.

Catching the criminal:

▶ Almost 100% of today's criminals are caught. Since the beginning of the century, our methods for catching criminals have improved. Criminals are no longer able to get away. Last year, there were only three unsolved crimes in our country.

▶ Computers have been programmed to develop profiles of criminals. All you have to do is give the computer a few clues–the damage, the way the criminal entered the house, the place and time of the crime, and the type of crime. Computers can identify the criminal's age, sex, hair color, eye color, height, weight, education, psychological characteristics, home town, and language. Computers can give us detailed information about the criminal's lifestyle. We can receive information about the criminal's friends and habits in no time at all.

▶ Recently, we have taught computers to name criminals and report where they are.

Punishing the criminal:

▶ We have done away with all old-fashioned punishments. The death penalty was abolished in 2005. All prisons were closed in 2017.

▶ We have developed electronic monitoring systems which control criminals in their homes. As you know, every criminal must wear an electronic bracelet at all times. These bracelets give a signal when the criminal steps out of the house.

▶ We have also developed a 24-hour-a-day electronic house monitoring system. Our monitors don't bother the criminals or their families. Our microphones and cameras hear and see through walls from many miles away, so criminals and their families can go on living normally.

▶ Prisons are not necessary even for very dangerous criminals. In some special cases, we have an electrode that can force the person back home. I am proud to report that we haven't had to use these electrodes since 2014.

The following was taken from the article "Moral Punishments" written by Prof. Filosorez, professor of Philosophy, in response to the above report:

It is true that most criminals are now easily caught. It is true that we have won the war against crime. However, we must ask ourselves: What price have we paid for this success? We must give some thought to the new methods that we have developed. Are they fair? Don't they ignore the right to privacy? Do we have the right to monitor a person 24 hours a day? By doing this, don't we take away the person's freedom, just as our grandparents did in the past? Is it more humane to put electrodes in peoples' bodies than to send them to prison? If the electronic bracelet beeps every time a criminal steps out of the house, isn't the house a prison?

It is true that prisons were a very costly system. It is also true that nowadays we can protect the public at a lower cost. However, saving money is not the only problem we must consider. Prof. Criminez ignores the moral problems that we must face. It is immoral to protect society at the cost of personal freedom. It is my belief that personal freedom is lost now just as much as it was lost in the past.

The time has come to find new ways to protect society. Modern technology may open new possibilities. We could send criminals to undersea cities or to space.

 Whose Point of View?

1. **Who agrees with the following statements? Prof. Criminez or Prof. Filosorez?**

    1. Prisons were a very costly system.
    2. Personal freedom was lost in the past.
    3. Personal freedom is lost now.
    4. The criminal's house is like a prison.
    5. The new methods are fair.
    6. Personal freedom should not be taken away from people.
    7. The criminal was treated like a disease.
    8. Some type of prison system is necessary.
    9. Criminals should be able to lead a normal life with their families.

2. **Prof. Criminez and Prof. Filosorez think some of the following methods are acceptable.** Who thinks so? **Prof. Criminez** or **Prof. Filosorez?**

    a. prisons
    b. death penalty
    c. electronic bracelets
    d. putting electrodes in people's bodies
    e. house monitoring
    f. sending criminals to undersea cities or to space

3. Add three more ideas.

4. Identify your own Point of View
What do **you** think?
- a. Does society have a right to punish criminals?
- b. Is it better to be imprisoned at home than in jail? Why do think so?
- c. Is it better to send criminals to space than to keep them in their homes? Why do you think so?

5. List three kinds of punishment that you think are fair. They can be well-known, or you may invent your own. Be prepared to argue in favor of your ideas.

> To refute means to argue against somebody else's arguments and to prove that they are wrong. Sometimes the writer agrees with a small part of the other's argument, but disagrees with the rest of it.

Read the following:

Agreement: It is true that most criminals are now easily caught.[56]

Disagreement: However, we must ask ourselves: What price have we paid for this success?

Agreement: It is true that prisons were a very costly system. It is also true that we can protect the public at a lower cost nowadays.

Disagreement: However, saving money is not the only problem we must consider. It is immoral to protect society at the cost of personal freedom.

 Choose two of the points that you disagreed with in "Whose Point of View" on the previous page and refute them.

You may begin like this:

It is true that / We have to accept the fact that / I agree that / We can't deny that...

And you may continue like this:

However / Nevertheless / But we shouldn't forget that...

 Two Sides to an Issue

Identify an article or a number of articles in a newspaper with arguments on one controversial issue from different points of view. Identify the arguments and their refutations. Students identify the points of view expressed by each person in the story (article) or each author. Students decide which side they agree with, thus identifying their own bias.

 **Three Sides To A Story**

Read the following. Who are the speakers?

_____:I was trying to talk to my relative, who is a new immigrant from Russia. We were really having trouble understanding each other. He was trying to make me understand something. He was very excited. He was making wild movements and hitting me on the shoulder. A woman was watching us from her window, and she seemed very interested in the conversation. I realized that she could understand Russian, so I asked her if she would mind translating for me. She slammed the window in my face. That goes to show you how rude and nasty people are. Nobody cares about anyone anymore.

_____:Two people were standing on the corner. They were shouting violently. I was looking out of my window and watching them when one of them noticed me. He seemed very excited. "Do you speak Russian?" he shouted at me. "Yes," I answered. I was sorry to find myself involved in their fight. I hate violence, so I shut the window and pulled down the shade.

_____:I was walking down the street when I suddenly saw my cousin. What an unexpected meeting! We were having a lot of trouble communicating, because my cousin doesn't speak Russian. A woman was watching us from her window. My cousin spoke to her, but she obviously hated immigrants, so she slammed the window in our faces. Do you see what it is like to be a new immigrant? What a way to greet newcomers! Do you see what we have to handle?

Each person understood the situation differently. What really happened? Complete the following passage to find out.

POST READING

Words to help you:

care, Russia, excited, fight, hated, immigrant, language,
not, relatives, rude, shut, speak, watching

Two people met in the street. They were **1**_____. Their meeting was unexpected, so they were very **2**_____. One of them
was a new **3**_____ from **4**_____. He did not speak our
5_____. The other one had forgotten how to **6**_____ Russian.
They could **7**_____ understand each other.

A woman was **8**_____ them from her window. She thought that
they were having a **9**_____, so she **10**_____ her window. The
first man thought that she was very **11**_____. He thought that
people don't **12**_____ about each other anymore. His relative
thought that she shut the window because she **13**_____ immigrants. [57]

SAMPLE ACTIVITY

AWARENESS OF WRITER'S MOOD

1. Is the writer happy or sad about his/her news? Underline words that show how the writer feels about the news.

Dear Bob,

*I'm sorry to say that things aren't going the way I planned
them. I hope you aren't too disappointed. I won't be able to
come to visit this summer. My mother thinks I should stay
home. I know I'll spend a boring summer, but I'm tired of
fighting with my parents. I'll write again tomorrow. Right
now, I'm too upset.*

Love,
Ann

Dear Sue,

Guess what? I have the measles! I'm going to spend the week in bed. This is all a terrible dream. It's the most disappointing thing. I am going to miss the opportunity of my life. Instead of winning a swimming medal, I'll be taking medicine. I miss you. Write to cheer me up.

Love,
Mark

Dear Sally,

I can't believe it! Finally! I was accepted. I am going to start practicing next week. It's all so exciting! This is a fantastic moment in my life. I can't wait to begin. In August we are going to play a game in Europe. What an opportunity! I miss you. Write soon.

Best regards,
Judy

Dear John,

Guess what? I'm coming to visit you this summer! Mom agrees because my report card was OK. Won't that be fun? Please start making plans. Write soon,

Love,
Betty

2. Complete the table. Compare Betty's letter to Ann's letter.

	Betty's Letter	Ann's Letter
positive words used		
negative words used		
mood		
plans for the summer		

3. Pretend you are Judy or Mark. Rewrite his or her letter and change the mood.

4. Write a letter to a friend. Don't tell your friend if you are happy or sad, but try to make him/her understand.

Dear _____,

I'm _____ to say that_____.

I'm going to _____. It's all_____.

This is the most _____in my life.

I hope that _____.

Love,

58

_____

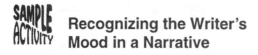

SAMPLE ACTIVITY   Recognizing the Writer's Mood in a Narrative

Read the text that follows.

Her Dream Came True

Mrs. Miller had a dream. In her dream she was a great singer. She wanted to sing in front of an audience. She could imagine the audience applauding and throwing flowers at her feet after every song. She imagined fantastic reviews about herself in all the newspapers.

In real life, Mrs. Miller was a hard-working woman. She knew that she didn't really have a great voice. In fact, she couldn't sing very well! She knew she couldn't be a star.

Mrs. Miller decided to make her dream come true. Every month she saved some money. After 20 years she had enough money to hire the biggest concert hall in New York.

She invited all her friends, relatives and neighbors. She sent invitations to many newspapers and TV reporters. When the great day came, the concert hall was full. Five thousand people came to hear Mrs. Miller sing! There were TV cameras and photographers everywhere. Mrs. Miller sang for 3 hours. Radio and TV stations reviewed her concert the following day. Mrs. Miller didn't become a great star, but she became famous!

 POST READING   **1. Mrs. Miller's dream was a happy dream.**

Read the first paragraph again and mark the words that show it was a good dream.

2. Make some changes in the paragraph and see what happens.
Fill in the blanks with your own words.

Mrs. Miller had a dream. In her dream she was a

_____ singer. She wanted to sing in front of an

audience. She could imagine the audience _____ing

and throwing _____ at her feet after every song.

She imagined _____ reviews about herself in all

the newspapers.

Is Mrs. Miller's dream still a happy one? Is it worth working and saving for 20 years to make it come true? [59]

▶▶▶ INSIGHTS ◀◀◀

In these activities students are made aware of the tone of the passages and how it reflects the writer's mood or feelings.

AWARENESS OF CONNOTATIONS AND BIAS

One way of enhancing the students' awareness of bias is to bring to their attention the different connotations words have. The teacher may choose two reading passages dealing with a current controversial problem, each presenting a different point of view. These should be 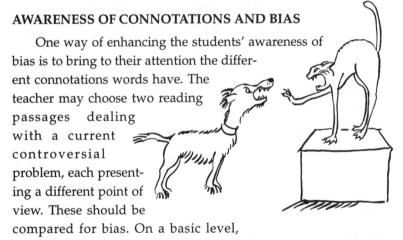 compared for bias. On a basic level, students may be asked to identify textual clues (words expressing bias, verbs of opinion, adjectives, subjective tone) that help them identify bias. On a higher level the students can be asked to decide on the things the writer is for and the things she/he is against.

SAMPLE ACTIVITY *Word Connotations*

Present lists of words out of context. Have your students classify the words as positive (+), negative (-), or neutral (0). The following are examples of words taken from the reading passages below: dirty (-), vast (+), silent (+), waste (-), scientists (0), ordinary (0), pollution (-), station (0), building (0).

Then, have them read the two texts and answer the questions. Point out that the connotations of the words out of context may be different from the connotations of the same words in context.

SILENT POWER

An ordinary power station is a noisy, dirty building. Railway sidings surround the station, and trains clatter in and out, bringing coal or oil to use in the boilers. Smoke from the boilers pours from high chimneys, polluting the atmosphere. What a difference from a nuclear power station, which is silent and clean; yet, inside, vast amounts of energy are being released.

Power stations make electricity by producing heat to boil water and using the steam produced to power electric generators. Ordinary power stations burn coal, oil, or gas in a furnace. Nuclear power stations consume nuclear fuel in a reactor. The amount of heat produced is huge. A piece of nuclear fuel the size of a tennis ball produces as much heat as burning 50 railway cars of coal! To get all this heat, the fuel is simply fed into the reactor; basically, nothing more has to be done.

POST READING

1. a. What is the writer's attitude toward ordinary power stations?
   b. Underline words or expressions in the passage that support your answer.
2. a. What is the writer's opinion about nuclear power stations?
   b. Support your answer with evidence from the text.

NUCLEAR DEATH

Nuclear power stations are a hazard to humanity. There is no danger that they would blow up like an atomic bomb, but the reactor produces radioactivity–invisible rays that cause severe illness. The reactor has to be covered with heavy shielding to stop the rays from getting out. The waste products left over in the reactor when the nuclear fuel is used up are also radioactive. They have to be carefully removed and stored in heavy containers or deep pits. The radioactivity lasts for thousands of years, and so the containers or pits must never leak.

Nowadays, about one tenth of the world's electricity comes from nuclear power, but because of the tremendous dangers of nuclear energy, scientists are now working hard to try to find a safer method of producing energy. Many scientists believe that fusion power is the answer; this is the way the sun produces its heat and light.

POST READING

1. a. What is the writer's attitude towards nuclear power stations?

    b. Support your answer.

2. Compare the bias of the two writers.
    Who is in favor of nuclear power stations? Who is against them? What is your opinion? Who do you agree with? Why?

Suggestion for more advanced classes.
    Discuss nuclear accidents (such as Chernobyl or Three Mile Island) and their implications. How does an incident of this kind affect our bias towards nuclear energy? How did it affect neighboring countries? How did it affect the world? Do you think that as a result of incidents of this sort that fewer nuclear power stations will be built?

AWARENESS OF GENRE

Awareness of genre is of great significance for the critical reader. Different genres typically use different styles and registers. An expository text is usually more formal than a narrative, a formal letter, as its title suggests, is more formal than a friendly letter. Moreover, they use various rhetorical functions and sometimes stereotypical language for different purposes in different situations.

Genres cannot be distinguished from one another on the basis of language alone. There are few linguistic markers that make one text expository and the other narrative. However, the general "feel" of the sophisticated reader is a good indication for genre. It is this "feel" that we should try to instill in our readers, so that when beginning to read a text, they know what genre it belongs to.

 SAMPLE ACTIVITY **These three passages are about animals and the way they learn.** Read them and decide where each passage is from.

> ▶ a children's magazine
>
> ▶ a science magazine
>
> ▶ a letter between friends

CAN ANIMALS THINK?

Thinking means being able to find solutions to new problems. Experiments show that animals can think. In one experiment, a monkey was in a room where a banana was hanging. It could not reach it. There were two boxes in the room. The monkey sat and looked at the banana and the boxes. Then it got up, placed one box on top of the other, climbed up and got the banana! The monkey was thinking!

However, most animals probably don't think as people do. They behave by instinct. They continue behaving the way their ancestors did. A dog barks at a strange sound–this is instinct. If a dog falls into the water, it will swim by instinct.

Other animals learn how to swim. They do not swim by instinct, but as a result of education. Some animals teach their young. Lions and tigers teach their babies to hunt. Bears teach babies to be quiet when they hunt.

Some animals can learn by imitation. They imitate their mother or other animals. For example, young chimpanzees learn how to break off branches, pull off leaves, and then use the branches to fish by watching their parents. The older animal is the model.

There is a need for further research to learn more about the ways that animals learn.

Where is this passage from?

ANIMAL TRAINERS

I'm finding out about animals from my neighbor Doris. Do you know what she does? She trains wild animals to perform in movies and on TV! Can you imagine? She trains lions, baboons, orangutans, snakes, and even spiders. How do you train a spider? According to Doris, first you try to win its love and trust. Doris praises her animals and gives them food when they do what she wants. So, stop hitting Lassie! Praise works better than punishment.

Remember that movie we saw last year, about the gorilla that attacked people? Doris trained the gorilla. Can you believe it? Doris is short, and she weighs about 115 pounds or 52 kilos!

Where is this passage from?

TALKING TO ANIMALS

Kanzi is a chimpanzee who doesn't look special. He's about three feet or one meter tall. He climbs trees and eats bananas like all chimpanzees, but he's really very special. Kanzi is learning a language. His teacher is teaching him to use symbols to communicate with people.

Kanzi cannot speak. He uses symbols and gestures to communicate. His teacher uses symbols on cards to talk to him. She touches the card to communicate with him.

Kanzi always wants water before he goes to bed. He usually touches the water card to ask for water. One day his teacher brought him ice water. He was so pleased that the next night he touched the water card and the ice card. Kanzi had created his own message!

Where is this passage from?

ENHANCING READING COMPREHENSION

POST READING

How did you decide?

	science magazine	children's magazine	letter
1. Which passage is the easiest?			
2. Which passage uses the longest words?			
3. Which passage uses the longest sentences?			
4. Which passage has the most facts?			
5. Which is the funniest?			
6. In which passage are things explained the most carefully?			
7. In which passage are there the most details?			
8. Which passage sounds the friendliest?			

60

▶▶▶ INSIGHTS ◀◀◀

The purpose of this activity is to make learners aware of style and language features that are typical of different genres. The activity following the passages may be attempted while reading to help learners who cannot make up their minds. Learners may discuss the style of texts in their own language and decide whether the criteria that are mentioned in the activity apply.

THE FORCE

On Monday, July 13, 1993, the "force" made its first appearance at the Tanners' house in Lake Forest, Indiana. Lights turned on and off by themselves. The radio and microwave oven turned themselves on. The shower began running even though there was no one in the bathroom, and the TV made noises although it was turned off.

The family soon understood that the "force" acted only when fourteen-year-old Ellen was around. Ellen Tanner performed a number of strange and mysterious actions. She made candlesticks roll across the room, caused the phone to fly above the sofa, and forced the hall lamp to swing back and forth. It seemed that Ellen had a special influence over the movement of objects.

Other people soon heard about the "force," and one day more than 30 friends and relatives came together to watch objects fly around Ellen's house. Two religious groups came to the house. They believed a supernatural force was responsible for the strange happenings. They tried to get rid of it, but they were unsuccessful.

On August 19th, 1993, a TV station videotaped Ellen near a "flying" lamp. When played back in slow motion, the video showed Ellen using her hand to move the lamp by its cord. Many people thought that this was proof of fraud. It seemed to them that Ellen was simply an excellent magician. But one parapsychologist who has studied Ellen's psychic abilities insists that Ellen really has the "force."

In 1994, a special committee was sent to Lake Forest to investigate the case. They studied photographs which appear to show a phone flying through the air. They concluded that "Ellen actually threw the phone across the room."

The parapsychologist, who does not believe these conclusions, continues to insist on Ellen's unusual powers.

"Ellen's powers are frightening," he says, "and I fear for her safety. Once she was sitting on the arm of a chair with her arms towards me when I saw the sofa "attack" her. It slid eighteen inches, and I was afraid it would hurt her legs. I also saw the phone fly at least seven times. A couple of times it hit Ellen so hard she screamed."

Ellen's mother says that a lot of damage, such as holes in the walls and doors, is caused by the objects that fly around the family's house.

The mystery of Ellen's special powers is still being investigated. Some scientists claim that Ellen, like others in the past, is just a magician. Others hope that they have discovered a new force that human beings can study and develop. They believe that if people had such a force, the future would hold new and exciting possibilities.

POST READING

1. Where do you expect to find a passage like this?
Choose the most likely answers.

    a. In a daily newspaper

    b. In a magazine for women

    c. In a psychology book

    d. In an encyclopedia

    e. In a science fiction book

    f. In a scientific government report

    g. In a children's magazine

    h. In a religious journal

    i. In a gossip magazine

2. Do you think this story is based on a real event? Why or why not?

3. The author wanted you to believe that this story was true.
Which elements did she include in the story to make it sound true? Write one example for each.

a. dates
b. detailed description of events
c. expert opinions
d. other people's opinions
e. eye witnesses' reports
f. long words
g. names of places
h. names of people
i. names of professions
j. quotations
k. reports of scientific investigations
l. presentation of more than one explanation
m. names of important people and organizations
n. scientific language

THE FORCE 2

I couldn't stand it for another minute. Ellen was only fourteen, but she was causing the TV to turn off again. Our lives were becoming impossible. Ellen was sitting on the sofa laughing with satisfaction. Jimmy was crying. "I hate you!" he shouted at Ellen. A plate hit Jimmy's shoulder. Ellen was using the "force." Without moving, she had caused the plate to fly across the room and hit Jimmy.

I looked at my daughter. Three weeks ago she woke up and suddenly announced that she had the force. I laughed at her and told her to stop trying to get attention. I'd had enough of her bragging. Ellen looked at me and smiled. "I'll prove it," she said. That night I heard the water on in the shower at midnight. I went into the shower. The water stopped. I turned to walk out, feeling upset. Before I could close the door, the water was running again. I stood thinking. The water stopped and started again before my eyes. I turned around and saw Ellen watching me with a triumphant smile on her face. "Well, Dad?" she said. "I guess I have the force after all."

"What are you talking about?" I said sadly. "Go to bed."

"Just a minute, Dad," Ellen said. "The bed will come to me."

I knew that Ellen wasn't joking. If she couldn't make the bed fly through the walls, at least she thought she could. I didn't want to find out. The next day Ellen caused objects to fly, roll, and whiz through the house. My heart was heavy. How could I face the future? I noticed Jimmy was staring at Ellen. Their eyes met and held. It seemed as if a kind of electricity was passing through the air. "Ah, hah!" said Jimmy "That's how you do it!"

"Boom." Suddenly the book I was holding flew out of my hand and hit Ellen on the head.

"Stop this right now!" I shouted angrily.

"Can't you see, Dad?" Ellen was very upset. "Jimmy has the force, too. Why does he have to copy everything I do?"

I sat down. I didn't want to understand what was happening, but I knew that I had to face the truth. My children were growing up. They already had the force. Pretty soon they would be able to leave the planet and go off on their own.

 POST READING 1. **Which elements are included in the story?**

a. dates

b. a plot

c. names of places

d. names of people

e. points of view

f. quotations

g. descriptions of how people feel

h. long words

i. expert opinions

j. eye witnesses' reports

k. a surprise ending

l. explanations

m. description of events

n. suspense

o. conversations between people

2. **What are the main differences between a report of an event and a short story? Compare this story to the report, "The Force." Discuss.** [61]

 ▶▶▶ INSIGHTS ◀◀◀

These activities are meant to make students aware of the difference between a fictitious story and a factual report. They are made aware of style and language features that are typical of different genres. The activities demonstrate what writers do in order to achieve credibility and why a story sounds real if it includes certain elements.

 **Changing Genre**

Choose a news item or any other suitable text, and rewrite it in a different genre. You may assign a different format to different groups or individual students.

Possible genres:

- ▶ a fictional story
- ▶ a short scientific article
- ▶ a process that one can follow
- ▶ a play
- ▶ a film script
- ▶ a dialogue among the participants
- ▶ a comic strip
- ▶ a historical report to be read 100 years from now

- slogans to be carried at a demonstration
- a descriptive report
- an interpretive report
- a critical report
- an editorial
- a song
- a photo or a picture
- an adventure game

Glossary

▶ ▶

Reading Comprehension terms as used in this book

abstract - a short summary including the main points of a piece of writing. An abstract usually precedes the passage.

anaphora - rhetorical device of cross-referencing words or phrases. (cf. reference words) e.g. Where are my glasses? I can't find *them.*

anticipation - mental process which allows readers to predict what is likely to happen based on minimal information about the text.

bias - a series of opinions constituting someone's point of view. A person's bias may interfere with his/her objectivity.

cloze - text-based, gap-filling activity.

cognitive processes - mental processes that are representative of our knowledge and ability to learn and allow us to comprehend texts.

coherence - means by which ideas, concepts, and propositions in a text are made to belong conceptually to the whole.

cohesion - linguistic means by which elements of a text are arranged and connected.

cohesive markers - words which signal logical relationships in a text.

connotation - the emotive and associative meaning of a word or words.

contextual clues - facts, ideas, and/or signal words that can be found in the text and suggest possible solutions to certain problems.

to deduce - to arrive at a conclusion by reasoning, using the facts available.

discourse cloze - gap-filling activity which taps whole text comprehension.

to evaluate - to make personal decisions and/or arrive at value judgments by considering alternatives.

expectation - what a reader thinks will happen or come next in the text based on the information available.

explicit information - information that is clearly and fully presented in the text.

expository text - text which presents theories, ideas, or facts. (cf. narrative)

extra-textual information - information outside the text that can help us understand the text or make correct predictions as to its contents.

generalization - broad explicit statement of principles and/or ideas that invite support of details.

genre - kind of text using characteristic style and register, e.g., expository, narrative, poetry, journalistic prose.

gist - the core or substance of a text.

heuristics - mental procedures that allow guessing, inferencing, predicting, etc.

implication - the relationship between two propositions and/or the conclusion drawn from that relationship.

implicit information - information that can be understood from a text although it is not overtly stated by the author. (cf. explicit information)

inference - logical conclusion derived from the explicit material in the text.

to internalize - to learn; to incorporate something into one's thinking processes.

lexis - the full vocabulary of a language.

main idea - the most important point or thought of a paragraph or text.

narrative - a story or account of events in writing.

prediction - the act of stating what one believes will happen in the text, anticipation.

procedure - sequence of steps to be followed in a teaching situation.

proposition - a full idea in sentence or clause form.

reference word - a word or expression that refers to and substitutes for another word or expression mentioned elsewhere in the text.

refutation - argument that proves that another argument is wrong.

scanning - making a rapid examination of a text in order to extract specific information from it.

sequencing - chronological, causal or any other logical order of ideas or concepts in a text.

skill - ability or proficiency in reading that comes from practice or experience in the use of various strategies. (cf. strategy)

skimming - making a rapid examination of a text in order to extract the main points from it, surveying, assessing.

strategy - a series of directed steps or "text attack" techniques to be followed by readers in order to comprehend a text.

summary cloze - gap-filling activity done as post reading and tapping comprehension of the main ideas of a text.

text mapping - text charting or condensation of a text and presentation in graphic mode.

topic - the subject of a paragraph or passage.

universe of texts - textual and non-textual information that constitutes a whole.

Appendix

▶ ▶

The following are suggested procedures that can be used for teaching some of the skills included in this book. They are only samples intended to show that there can be a logical sequence in the reading comprehension lesson. Similar procedures can be applied to other skills and strategies.

COPING WITH WORD MEANINGS
For exercises see Ch. 5, Guessing Word Meanings

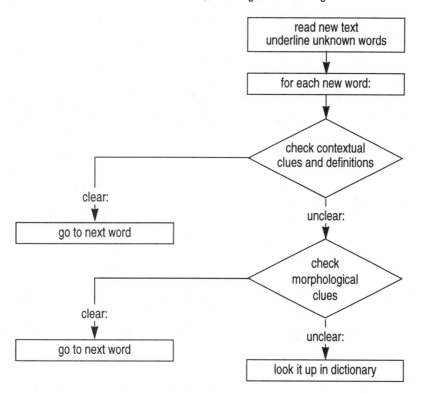

This is the suggested procedure for dealing with new lexical items. It should be made clear to students, however, that it is often possible to understand a text in spite of a few unknown lexical items.

PREDICTION (Option 1)
For exercises see Ch. 5, Prediction as a Means to Comprehension

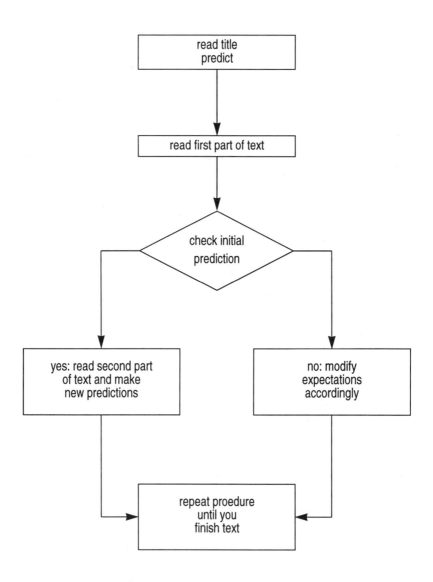

read title
predict

read first part of text

check initial
prediction

yes: read second part
of text and make
new predictions

no: modify
expectations
accordingly

repeat proedure
until you
finish text

PREDICTION (Option 2)

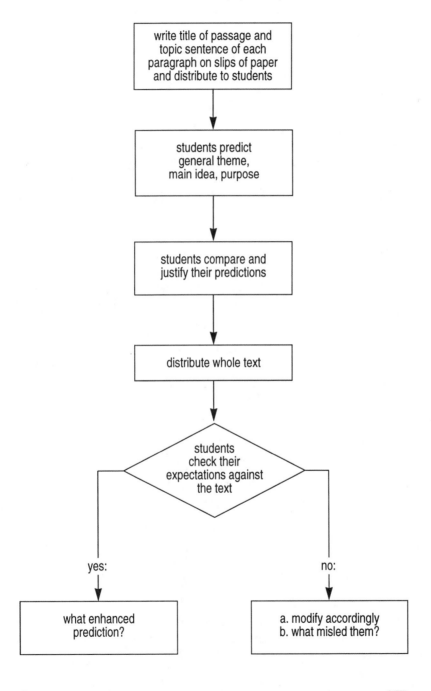

write title of passage and topic sentence of each paragraph on slips of paper and distribute to students

↓

students predict general theme, main idea, purpose

↓

students compare and justify their predictions

↓

distribute whole text

↓

students check their expectations against the text

yes: → what enhanced prediction?

no: → a. modify accordingly
b. what misled them?

EVALUATION - INDUCTIVE PATH

For exercises cf. Ch. 8, Processes of Evaluation

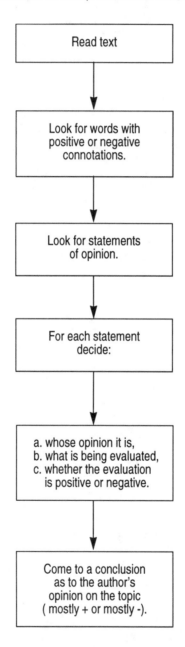

Read text

Look for words with
positive or negative
connotations.

Look for statements
of opinion.

For each statement
decide:

a. whose opinion it is,
b. what is being evaluated,
c. whether the evaluation
   is positive or negative.

Come to a conclusion
as to the author's
opinion on the topic
(mostly + or mostly -).

EVALUATION - DEDUCTIVE PATH

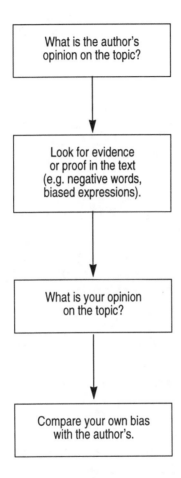

What is the author's opinion on the topic?

↓

Look for evidence or proof in the text (e.g. negative words, biased expressions).

↓

What is your opinion on the topic?

↓

Compare your own bias with the author's.

Index

Sources

▶ ▶

THE FOLLOWING is a list of the sources of the many excercises presented in this book. Those excercises not listed were developed by the authors specifically for this book.

By consensual agreement, many of the author's examples have been taken from *The Junior Files Series,* also published by Alta Book Center, Publishers. For ease of reference, *Junior Files, File 1: English for Today* (1991) is abbreviated *JF1,; Junior Files, File 2: English for Tomorrow* (1993) is abbreviated *JF2;* and *The English Files: English for Tomorrow and Beyond* (1995) is abbreviated *EF.*

1. JF1, p. 137.*

2. EF, pp. 153 - 154.

3. EF, p. 142.

4. EF, p. 143.

5. JF2 p. 117.

6. JF2 pp. 118 - 119.

7. Fillmore, C. J., 1981. "Ideal readers and real readers." In D. Tannen, Ed., *Georgetown University Roundtable on Langauge and Linguistics.* 248-270, Washington, D.C. USA: Georgetown University Press.

8. Sanford, A. J. and Garrod, S.C., 1981. *Understanding Written Language: Explorations of Comprehension Beyond the Sentence.* New York, USA: John Wiley.

9. JF2 pp. 47 - 48.

10. EF, p. 11.

11. JF2 pp. 190 - 191.

12. JF2 p. 44.

13. JF2 p. 45.

14. EF, p. 171.

15. JF2 pp. 126 - 127.

16. JF2 p. 22.

17. EF, pp. 26 - 31.

18. JF2 pp. 244 - 245.

19. EF, pp. 144 - 145.

20. EF, p. 245.

21. JF2 pp. 215 - 216.

22. JF2 pp. 234 - 235.

23. JF1, pp. 37 - 38.

24. EF, p. 172.

25. JF1, pp. 194 - 195.

26. JF2 p. 128.

27. JF2 pp. 137 - 138.

28. JF2 pp. 61 - 62.

29. JF2 p. 221.

30. JF2 p. 40.

31. EF, p. 13.

32. EF, pp. 146 - 148.

33. EF, p. 226.

34. EF, p. 298.

35. JF2 pp. 60 - 62.

36. JF1, p. 105.

37. JF2 pp. 233 - 234.

38. EF, pp. 96 - 97.

39. EF, p. 309.

40. JF1, pp. 11 - 12.

41. JF2 p. 222.

42. EF, p. 67.

43. JF1, pp. 134 - 135.

44. EF, pp. 201 - 205.

45. EF, p. 200.

46. EF, p. 245.

47. JF2 pp. 84 - 86.

48. EF, pp. 253 - 255.

49. EF, pp. 263 - 265.

50. JF2 pp. 48 - 49.

51. EF, p. 15.

52. JF1, pp. 9 - 10.

53. JF1, pp. 52 - 54.

54. JF2 p. 12.

55. EF, p. 252.

56. EF, pp. 102 - 103.

57. EF, p. 149.

58. JF1, pp. 152 - 153.

59. JF1, pp. 118 - 120.

60. EF, pp. 187 - 190.

61. EF, pp. 19 - 20.

62. JF2 pp. 228 - 229.

63. JF2 pp. 90 - 91.

64. JF2 pp. 58 - 59.

65. EF, pp. 54 - 59.